TALES OF
THE ANGLER'S ELDORADO
NEW ZEALAND

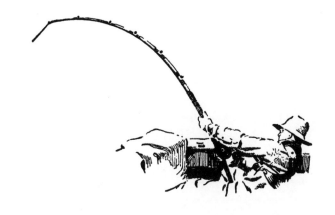

CAMP AT BAY OF ISLANDS

PLATE I

Tales of The
Angler's Eldorado, New Zealand

by

ZANE GREY

THE DERRYDALE PRESS
LANHAM AND NEW YORK

THE DERRYDALE PRESS

Published in the United States of America
by The Derrydale Press
4720 Boston Way, Lanham, Maryland 20706

Distributed by NATIONAL BOOK NETWORK, INC.
Copyright © 1953 by Zane Grey
First Derrydale printing with french folds 2000

Library of Congress Cataloging-in-Publication Data

Grey, Zane, 1872-1939.
　　Tales of the Angler's Eldorado, New Zealand / by Zane Grey.
　　　　p.　cm.
　　Originally published : 1st ed. New York : Harper & Brothers, 1926.
　　ISBN 978-1-58667-029-0
　　1. Big game fishing—New Zealand.　I. Title

SH678.G5 2000
799.1'0993—dc21　　　　　　　　　　　　　　　00-035839

I gratefully dedicate this book

To

C. ALMA BAKER,

who first fired me with a longing to visit New Zealand and
fish in its purple unknown waters.

To

A. H. MESSENGER AND EARNEST WIFFIN,

who helped so inspiringly and materially to make my trip a success.

To

A. N. BRECKON,

whose splendid photographs verify in some degree the tremendous claim
this book makes for New Zealand.

To

CYRIL MONTAGUE MORTON,

cinematographer extraordinary, who braved the rough seas, day after day,
week after week, always on deck with his motion-picture camera,
always ready with his cheery call—
"When do we eat?
When do we eat?
When do we eat?"

To

CAPTAIN LAURIE D. MITCHELL,

who takes place next my brother R. C. as patient, following, long-suffering,
loyal fishing comrade, whose low thrilling chant
will always fill my angling dreams—
"I got a bite!
I got a bite!
I got a bite!"

To

FRANCIS ARLIDGE,

the boy-wonder engineer and boatman, whose
engine obeyed word of command, whose
wheel needed not the help of steering eyes.

To

PETER WILLIAMS,

whaler, the best and coolest and strongest man
who ever stood at my side with a gaff.

To

LEON WARNE AND BILL HODGSON,
who manned the Captain's boat, drank gallons of tea
and saw millions of imaginary fins.
And lastly

To

HOKA DOWN,
Maori guide of the Tongariro, whose big heart shone in his ever-ready smile,
and who instilled in me the fishing faith of his forefathers.

ZANE GREY

Avalon, California.
May, 1926

ILLUSTRATIONS

ILLUSTRATIONS

CHAPTER I

THERE is always something so wonderful about a
new fishing adventure trip. For a single day, or
for a week, or for months! The enchantment never
palls. Years on end I have been trying to tell why, but
that has been futile. Fishing is like Jason's quest for the
Golden Fleece.

The most humble fisherman has this in common with
fishermen of all degrees. Whatever it is that haunts
and enchants surely grows with experience. Even the
thousandth trip to the same old familiar fished-out
stream begins with renewed hope, with unfailing faith.
Quien sabe? as the Spaniards say. You cannot tell what
you might catch. And even if you do not catch anything
the joy somehow is there. The child is father to the man.
Saturdays and vacation times call everlastingly to the
boy. The pond, the stream, the river, the lake and the
sea! Something evermore is about to happen. Every
fishing trip is a composite of all other trips; and it holds
irresistible promise for the future. That cup cannot be
drained. There are always greater fish than you have

caught, always the lure of greater task and achievement, always the inspiration to seek, to endure, to find, always the beauty of the lonely stream and open sea; always the glory and dream of nature.

When I fished under the stark lava slopes of the Galapagos and in the amethyst waters around Cocos Island and around the White Friars I imagined each was the epitome of angling; that I could never adventure higher and farther! But in this same year 1925, when we shot the wild rapids of the Rogue River and cast our flies where none save Indians had ever fished, the same elusive and beautiful thing beckoned like a will-o'-the-wisp. It is in the heart.

On December thirtieth, when Captain Laurie Mitchell and I stood on the deck of the Royal Mail S.S. *Makura*, steaming out through the Golden Gate bound for the Antipodes to seek new waters, the same potent charm pervaded my being. There was a Lorelei calling from the South Seas; there was a siren bell ringing from the abysmal deep.

San Francisco Bay at that hour was a far cry from the turquoise-blue water of the tropics. A steely sun made pale bright light upon the ruffled bay; gay fog shrouded the dome of Mt. Tamalpais; from the northwest a cold wind drove down on the bare brown hills to whip the muddy water into a choppy sea. The broken horizon line of the beautiful city of hills shone dark against the sky. A flock of screaming gulls sailed and swooped about the stern of the vessel.

A big French freighter kept abreast of the *Makura* through the Golden Gate, then turned north, while we headed to the southwest. The Royal Mail ship *Makura* was no leviathan, but she certainly was a greyhound of the sea. In less than an hour I saw the mountains fade into the fog. That last glimpse of California had to

The Grassy Slopes of Orupukupuku Island

PLATE II

WINDING OFF FISHING LINE TO DRY

PLATE III

suffice me for a long time. We ran into a heavy ridged sea, cold and dark, with sullen whitecaps breaking. I walked the decks, watching as always, until the sky became overspread with dark clouds, and a chill wind drove me inside.

That night after dinner I went out again. The sky was dark, the sea black, except for the pale upheavals of billows which gleamed through the obscurity. The ship was rushing on, now with a graceful, slow forward dip, and then with a long rise. She was very steady. Great swells crashed against her bows and heaved back into the black gulfs. There was a continuous roar of chafing waters. An old familiar dread of the ocean mounted in me again. What a mighty force! It was a cold wintry almost invisible sea, not conducive to the thrill and joy of the angler. It was a northern sea, gusty, turbulent, with rough swells. I leaned over the rail in the darkness, trying to understand its meaning, its mood, trying to be true to the love I bore it in tranquil moments.

Next morning when I went out the decks were wet, the sky gray except low down in the east where rays of sunlight slipped through to brighten the cold gray buffeting sea.

I noted several sea birds following in the wake of the ship. They were new to me. Dark in color, marvelously built, with small compact bodies, sharp as a bullet, and with long narrow wings, they appeared to have been created for perfect control of the air. They sailed aloft and swooped down, skimmed the foamy crests, rode abreast of the rough seas, and dipped into the hollows, all apparently without slightest effort of wing. I did not see them flap a wing once. This is a common habit of many sea birds, especially the shearwaters, but I had never before seen it performed so swiftly and wonderfully. These birds had a wing spread of three feet, and must have belonged to the shearwater family. Lonely wanderers of the barren waste of waters!

Morning and afternoon swiftly passed, the hours flying with the speed of the *Makura* over the waves. Toward sunset, which was only a dim ruddy glow behind the fog banks, the chill wind, the darkening sea, the black somber fading light all predicted storm. The last daylight hours of the last day of 1925 were melancholy and drear. I was reminded of November back in Lackawaxen, Pennsylvania, where so often I heard the autumn winds wail under the eaves, and the rain pelt the roof—mournful prelude to winter.

This rough sea was like that of the north, where off the rugged shores of Puget Sound the contending tides are raw and bold. The winter twilight quickly merged into the blanket of night. Then out there in the opaque blackness the sea roared by the ship, tremendous and inscrutable, with nothing to inspire love, with everything to confound the soul of man. What was the old year to the sea, or the new year soon to dawn with its imagined promise, its bright face, its unquenchable hope? Nevertheless, the thought that overbalanced this depression was of the magic isles of the South Seas, set like mosaics in the eternal summer blue, and of the haunting Antipodes, seven thousand miles down the lanes of the Pacific.

All morning of the third day out the *Makura* sped on over a lumpy leaden sea, mirroring the gray of the sky. How tenaciously the drab shadow of winter clung to us! Yet there had come some degree of warmth, and on the afternoon of this day the cold wind departed. When the sunlight strayed through the fog, it gave the sea its first tinge of blue; but the sun shone only fitfully. There was no life on the sea, and apparently none in it. Neither bird nor fish showed to long-practiced eyes. I wondered about this. We were hundreds of miles offshore, out of the track of the schools of sardines and anchovies that birds and fish prey upon. Still there should have been some manifestation of life. How vast the ocean! Were its great open spaces and depths utterly barren? That was hard to believe.

Sunset that night was rose and gold, a gorgeous color thrown upon a thin webbed mass of mackerel cloud that for long held its radiance. It seemed to be a promise of summer weather. Sunrise next morning likewise was a blazing belt of gold. But these rich colorings were ephemeral and deceiving. The sky grew dark and gray. From all points masses of cumulous clouds rose above the horizon, at last to unite in a canopy of leaden tones. A wind arose and the sea with it. The air still had an edge.

All day the *Makura* raced over a magnificent sea of long swells rising to white breaking crests. The ship had a slow careen, to and fro, from side to side, making it difficult to walk erect and steadily. The turbulent mass of water was almost black. Its loneliness was as manifest as when calm. No sail! No smoke from steamer down beyond the horizon! No sign of fish or bird! I seemed to have been long on board. The immensity of the sea began to be oppressive. That day and the next we drove on over a gray squally expanse of waters.

The time came when I saw my first flying fish of the trip. It was an event. He appeared to be a tiny little fellow, steely in color, scarcely larger than a humming bird. But for me he meant life on the ocean. Thereafter while on deck I kept watch. We had sunshine for a few hours and then the warmth became evident. The sea was a raging buffeting rolling plain of dark blue and seething white. We were a thousand miles and more off the coast, where I felt sure the wind always blew. We were in the track of the trade winds.

On the sixth day the air became humid. We had

reached the zone of summer. Every mile now would carry us toward the tropics.

I saw some porpoises, small yellow ones, active in flight. They were a proof of fish, for porpoises seldom roam far away from their food supply. I wondered if they preyed upon the tiny flying fish. Swift as the porpoise is, I doubt that he could catch them. As we sped south I noted more and more schools of flying fish, rising in a cloud, like silvery swallows. Presently I espied one that appeared larger, with reddish wings. This was a surprise, and I thought I had made a mistake, as I had not a really good look at it. Not long afterward, however, I saw another, quite close, and made certain of the red wings. Then soon following I espied three more of the same species. They certainly could sail and glide and dart over the rough water.

We ran into a squall. Rain and spray wet my face as I paced the deck. Out ahead the gray pall was like a bank of fog. The sea became rougher. Our wireless brought news of a hurricane raging over the South Seas, centering around the Samoan Islands, where tidal waves had caused much damage. What had become of the tranquil Pacific? Late that afternoon we ran out of the squalls into a less-disturbed sea.

Captain Mitchell met two widely-traveled Englishmen on board, brothers, by name Radmore. They came from the same part of England where Captain Mitchell was born; and it must have been pleasant, as well as poignant, for him to talk with them. He introduced them to me, and I found them exceedingly interesting, as I have found so many Englishmen. I did not need to be told that they had been in the war.

I was particularly interested in their voyage to New Zealand, which was for the same purpose as ours—the wonderful possibilities of adventure, especially fishing, to be had in the Antipodes. The elder Radmore had been often to New Zealand, and in fact he knew Australasia, and island seas to the north. He was a big-game hunter, having had some extensive hunts in Burma, India, the Malay Peninsula, and British East Africa. He said game of all kinds had increased enormously during and since the war, especially in Africa. Tigers were abundant in Burma and seldom hunted. What the fishing possibilities might be in the waters adjacent to these places he had no idea. No sportsman had ever tried them. I conceived an impression of magnificent unknown virgin seas, so far as fish were concerned. What a splendid thrill that gave me!

Radmore told me many things, two of which I must chronicle here. The pearl fishing off the New Guinea coast! It was new pearl country, comparatively. In fact New Guinea is still one of the little-known islands. Next to Australia it is the largest in the world, and it has many leagues of unexplored coast line. Radmore told me that at one time rare pearls could be cheaply procured from the natives, who had not yet become aware of their value. A can of peaches bought a $16,000 pearl! The Radmores, coming into San Pedro on the S.S. *Manchuria*, had their attention called to my schooner *Fisherman* anchored in the bay. They said if they had that ship they would surely go to New Guinea.

On a voyage from New Zealand to England, round the Horn, Radmore had seen a remarkable battle between a sperm whale, or cachalot, and two great orcas. This conflict had taken place in smooth water close to a reef along which the ship was skirting. The whale was on the surface, apparently unable to sound, and he beat the water terrifically with his enormous flukes. The sound was exceedingly loud and continuous, almost resembling thunder. The orcas threw their huge white-and-black bodies high into the air, and plunged down upon the back of the whale. They hit with a sodden crash. The cachalot threshed with his mighty tail, trying to strike them, but they eluded it. The commotion in the water seemed incredible. This battle continued as long as the watchers could see with the naked eye, and then with glasses. The captain, who had sailed that route for forty years, said that was the third fight of the kind he had seen.

Radmore was certain the whale was a cachalot, or sperm. Personally, I incline to the opinion that it was some other kind of whale. Andrews and other authorities on whales claim that the whale-killers and orcas let the cachalot severely alone. He is more than a match for them. Armed with a terrible set of teeth and a head one-third the length of his ninety-foot body, the cachalot would appear to be impervious to attacks from sea creatures. On the other hand, other whales are helpless before the onslaught of these wolves of the sea. They become almost paralyzed with fright, and make little attempt to escape their foes. This is the naturalistic opinion on the subject, and I incline to it, although I admit a possibility of unusual cases. The wonderful thing about the narrative for me was to think of seeing such a battle and photographing it.

On the morning of January sixth before daybreak we crossed the equator. I went out on deck before sunrise. Sea and sky were radiant with a pearly effulgence. There were no reds, purples or golds. White and silver, gray and pearl predominated, which colors intensified as the sun came up, giving a beautiful effect. All around the horizon the trade-wind clouds rode like sails. They had the same ship-like shape, the same level bottoms and round wind-blown feathery margins as the trade-wind clouds above the Gulf Stream between Cuba and the

Keys; but not the color! Sunrise off the Keys of Florida is a glorious burst of crimson and gold that flames sky and sea.

We were now in the southern hemisphere, and I felt that it would be interesting for me to note the slow march of the sun to the north. On the equator the sun always sets at six o'clock. So far the voyage had been remarkably free of glaring white sunlight. This day when we crossed the equator we had alternately bright sunlight and soft gray-shaded sky.

Sometimes the ships of the Union Line pass within sight of the high peaks of the Marquesan Islands. I could not but feel what marvelous good fortune for me if that should be my lot! As it turned out, however, we did not pass close enough to the Marquesans to see them. I had to satisfy myself with the thrilling fact that somewhere short of a hundred miles beyond the horizon lay these gem-isles of the Pacific, alone amid the splendid solitude of this purple sea.

The night we entered the Paumotu Archipelago, or Low Islands, I had a striking sight of the planet Venus, so extraordinarily beautiful and incredibly bright in that latitude. The great star was exceedingly brilliant, yet not white; it had color, almost a gold or red, and left a shining track over the waters almost like that of the moon. Sometimes it seemed like a huge lantern hung close to the ship; again it retreated to the very rim of the world. Then how swiftly it went down into the sea! Another phenomenon I had noted lately was the singularly swift sunset, and the extreme brevity of light afterward.

There are two kinds of islands in the South Pacific, the low and the high. The former consist of atolls with their circular ridge of white sand above the coral, fringed with cocoanut palms; and the latter, mountains of volcanic origin, are characterized by high peaks densely over-grown with tropical verdure. The Paumotus are a vast aggregation of low islands, or atolls, sprinkled all over a great range of water. Yachts are forbidden to adventure in this perilous archipelago. The charts cannot be trusted, the currents are treacherous, the winds more contrary than anywhere else on the globe. Yet the course of the S.S. *Makura* ran straight through the archipelago. Probably many atolls were passed close at hand, wholly invisible from the deck; and it was only at the latter part of the long run through, that the course came anywhere near the clustered islands that gave the place its name.

CHAPTER II

MY FIRST and long-yearned-for sight of an atoll
came about mid-afternoon on January eighth. I
saw with naked eyes what most passengers were
using marine glasses to distinguish. It was a low fringe
of cocoanut-palm trees rising out of the blue sea. What
a singular first impression I had! Instantly it seemed I
was fishing off the Florida Keys, along the edge of the
Gulf Stream, and that I knew my location exactly because I could still see the cocoanut palms of Long Key.
I found myself saying, "They are about six miles in, unless these Pacific cocoanuts are much higher trees than
those of the Atlantic."

This islet, or atoll, was the first of many of the Paumotu Archipelago that were soon to rise gradually out
of the heaving blue floor of the ocean. They appeared
like green growths on a Hindu magician's carpet. Most
were small with just a few trees fringing the sky line;
but some were long and large, with thick groves of cocoanut palms. It was impossible, of course, to distinguish
these atolls from the Keys of the Florida Peninsula or

the islets of the Caribbean Sea. The great beauty of an atoll cannot be seen from afar. The ring of coral sand rising just above the sea, the ring of cocoanuts round it, the ring of turquoise-blue water inside, the ever-famed lagoon, blue as the sky, serene and tranquil, with its sands of gold and pearl, its myriads of colored fish, the tremendous thundering of the surf outside—these wonderful features could not be appreciated from the ship.

I went up on the third deck where I could see the strips of white beach and the bright green band of palms. These Paumotus surely called with all the mystery and glory of the South Pacific; but our ship passed swiftly on her way and soon night blotted out sight of the fascinating atolls.

Next morning I was up before dawn. The ship was moving very slowly. I could scarcely hear any sound of swirling waters. I went out on deck in the dim opaque gloom of a South Pacific dawn. The air was fresh, cool, balmy, laden with a scent of land. On the starboard side I saw a black mountain, rising sharp with ragged peaks. This island was Moorea, the first of the Society group.

Soon dead ahead appeared the strange irregular form of Tahiti. It made a marvelous spectacle, with the rose of the east kindling low down in a notch between two peaks. Tahiti was high. I watched the day come and the sun rise over this famous island, and it was indescribable. We went through a gateway in the barrier reef, where the swells curled and roared, and on into the harbor to the French port, Papeete.

Seen from the deck of a vessel Papeete was beautiful, green and luxurious, with its colored roofs, its blossoming trees, its schooners and other South Sea craft moored along the shore. The rise of the island, however, its ridged slopes of emerald green and amber red, its patches

CHOOSING A LEADER

PLATE IV

THE AUTHOR AT REAL WORK, NOT FISHING REEL

PLATE V

of palms, its purple canyons streaked with white waterfalls, its ragged, notched, bold peaks crowned with snowy clouds—these made a spectator forget that Papeete nestled at its base.

I spent a full day in this world-famed South Sea Island port, the French Papeete. It was long enough for me! Despite all I had read I had arrived there free of impressions, with eager receptive mind. I did not wonder that Robert Louis Stevenson went to the South Seas a romancer and became a militant moralist. It was not fair, however, to judge other places through contact with Papeete.

The French have long been noted for the careless and slovenly way in which they govern provinces. Papeete is a good example. There is no restriction against the Chinese, who appeared to predominate in business. Papeete is also the eddying point for all the riffraff of the South Seas. The beach comber, always a romantic if pathetic figure in my memory, through the South Sea stories I have read, became by actual contact somewhat disconcerting to me, and wholly disgusting. Perhaps I did not see any of the noble ruins.

Every store I entered in Papeete was run by a crafty-eyed little Chinaman. I heard that the Chinese merchants had all the money. It was no wonder. I saw very few French people. I met one kindly-looking priest. All the whites who fell under my gaze seemed to me to be sadly out of place there. They were thin, in most cases pale and unhealthy-looking. It was plain to me that the Creator did not intend white men to live on South Sea Islands. If he had he would have made the pigment of their skins capable of resisting the sun.

This was the early summer for Tahiti. It was hot. New York at 99 degrees in the shade, or Needles, California, at 115 degrees, would give some idea of heat at

Papeete! It was a moist sticky oppressive enervating heat that soon prostrated. I always could stand hot weather, and I managed to get around under this. But many of the ship passengers suffered, and by five o'clock that evening were absolutely exhausted.

What amazed me was the fact that this heat did not prevent the drinking of liquor. Champagne and other beverages were exceedingly cheap at Papeete. I found out long ago that a great many people who think they travel to see and learn really travel to eat and drink, and the close of this day on shore at Papeete provided a melancholy example of the fact. If I saw one bottle of liquor come aboard the S.S. *Makura* I saw a hundred. Besides such openly avowed bottles, there were cases and cases packed up in the companionway for delivery.

Captain Mitchell, Mr. Radmore and I visited the hotel or resort made famous mostly through Mr. O'Brien's book, *White Shadows of the South Seas.* Luxurious growths of green and wonderfully fragrant flowers surrounded this little low house of many verandas; but that was about all I could see attractive there. It appeared different classes of drinkers had different rooms in which to imbibe. Of those I passed, some approached what in America we would call a dive. It is all in the way people look at a thing. The licentiousness of women and the availability of wine rank high in the properties of renown.

The Tahitian women presented an agreeable surprise to me. From all the exotic photographs I had seen I had not been favorably impressed. But photographs do not do justice to Tahitian women. I saw hundreds of them, and except in a few cases, noticeably the dancers, who in fact were faked to impress the tourists, they were modestly dressed and graceful in appearance. They were strong, well built though not voluptuous, rather lightskinnéd and not at all suggesting negroid blood. They presented a new race to me. They had large melting melancholy eyes. They wore their hair in braids down their backs, like American schoolgirls of long ago when something of America still survived in our girls. These Tahitians had light-brown, sometimes nut-brown and chestnut hair, rich and thick and beautiful. What a delight to see! What pleasure to walk behind one of these barefooted and free-stepping maidens just for the innocent happiness of gazing at her wonderful braid! No scrawny shaved bristled necks, such as the flappers exhibit now, to man's bewildered disgust; no erotic and abnormal signs of wanting to resemble a male! Goodness only knows why so-called civilized white women of modern times want to look like men, but so it seems they do. If they could see the backs of the heads of these Tahitian girls and their long graceful braids of hair, that even a fool of a man could tell made very little trouble, and was so exquisitely feminine and beautiful, they might have a moment of illumined mind.

The scene at the dock as the S.S. *Makura* swung off was one I shall not soon forget. Much of Papeete was there, except, most significantly, the Chinese. No doubt they were busily counting the enormous number of French francs they had amassed during the day. The watchers in the background were quiet and orderly, and among these were French ladies who were bidding friends farewell, and other white people whose presence made me divine they were there merely to watch a ship depart for far shores. A ship they longed to be aboard! I could read it in their eyes.

In the foreground, however, were many Tahitian women and some half caste, with the loud-mouthed roustabouts who were raving at the drunken louts on board the ship. It was not a pretty sight. Near me on the rail sat an inebriated youth, decorated with flowers, waving a champagne bottle at those below. I did not see any friendliness in the uplifted dark eyes. This was only another ship going on down to the sea; and I thought most of those on board were held in contempt by those on land.

I did not leave Papeete, however, without most agreeable and beautiful impressions. Outside of the town there were the simplicity and beauty of the native habitations and the sweetness of the naked little Tahitians disporting on the beach. There were the magnificence of the verdure, foliage and flowers and the heavy atmosphere languorous with fragrance. There were the splendor of the surf breaking on the reef seen through the stately cocoanut palms, the burn of the sun and the delicious cool of the shade. There were the utter and ever-growing strangeness of the island and the unknown perceptions that were gradually building up an impression of the vastness of the South Sea. There were the splendor of Nature in her most lavish moods and the unsolvable mystery of human life.

I saw many old Tahitian men who I imagined had eaten human flesh, "long pig," as they called it in their day. The record seemed written in their great strange eyes.

Birds and fish were almost negligible at Tahiti. For all the gazing that I put in I saw only a few small needle fish. Not a shark, not a fin, not a break or swirl on the surface! There were no gulls, no sea birds of any kind, and I missed them very much. I saw several small birds about the size of robins, rather drab-colored with white on their wings, black heads and yellow beaks. They were tame and had a musical note.

On the next day out from Papeete we saw steamship smoke on the horizon. It grew into the funnel of a ship, then the hull, and at last the bulk of the sister ship of the *Makura*, the *Tahiti*. She passed us perhaps five miles away, a noble sight, and especially fascinating because she was the only traveling craft on our horizon throughout the voyage.

A little after daybreak on the following morning I was awakened by the steward, who said Roratonga was in sight. From a distance this island appeared to be a cone-shaped green mass rising to several high sharp-toothed peaks. Near at hand, in the glory of the sunrise, it looked like a beautiful mountain, verdant and colorful, rising out of a violet sea. I noted the extremely sharp serrated ridges rising to the peaks, all thickly covered with tropic verdure. The island appeared to be surrounded by a barrier reef, against which the heaving sea burst into white breakers.

Schools of flying fish, darting like swarms of silver bees, flew from before our bows. That was a promising sight, for usually where there are schools of small fish the great game fish will be found. Here, as at Tahiti, there was a marked absence of birds.

After Papeete, the weather was delightfully cool. The *Makura* anchored outside the reef, half a mile from shore, and small launches with canoe-shaped lighters carried cargo and passengers through a narrow gate in the reef to the docks.

Roratonga was under English control, and certainly presented an inspiring contrast to the decadent and vitiated Papeete. At once we were struck with the cleanliness of streets and wharfs, and the happy, care-free demeanor of the natives. They looked prosperous, and we were to learn that they all owned their bit of cocoanut grove and were independent. We drove around the island, a matter of twenty miles more or less. The road was level and shady all the way, with the violet white-wreathed sea showing through the cocoanut trees on one side and the wonderful sharp peaks rising above the forest on the other.

There were places as near paradise as it has been my good fortune to see. Flowers were as abundant as in a conservatory, with red and white blossoms prevailing. Children ran from every quarter to meet us, decorated with wreaths and crowns of flowers, and waving great bunches of the glorious bloom. They were bright-eyed merry children, sincere in their welcome to the visitors. Some of the native houses were set in open glades, where wide-spreading, fern-leaved trees blazing with crimson blossoms were grouped about the green shady lawns. The glamour of the beautiful colors was irresistible. The rich thick amber light of June in some parts of the United States had always seemed to me to be unsurpassable; but compared with the gold-white and rose-pink lights of Roratonga it grew pale and dull in memory. The air was warm, fragrant, languorous. It seemed to come from eternal summer. Everywhere sounded the wash of the surf on the reef. You could never forget the haunting presence of the ocean.

After our trip round the island we spent a couple of hours on the beach with the natives. This was in the center of the town. A continual stream of natives strolled and rode by. Their colored garments added to the picturesque attraction of the place. On the reef just outside could be seen the bones of a schooner sticking from the surface; and farther out the ironwork of a huge ship that had been wrecked there years ago. They seemed grim reminders of the remorselessness of the azure sea. The atmosphere of the hour was one of sylvan summer, the gentle and pleasant warmth of the South Seas, the idle happy tranquillity of a place favored by the gods; but only a step out showed the naked white teeth of the coral reef, and beyond that the inscrutable and changeful sea.

We bought from the natives until our limited stock of English money ran out. Then we were at the pains of seeing the very best of the pearls, baskets, bead necklaces and hatbands, fans and feathers, exhibited for our edification. These natives found their tongues after a while and talked in English very well indeed. What a happy contrast from the melancholy shadow-faced Tahitians!

It was interesting to learn that liquor is prohibited at Roratonga. If any evidence were needed in favor of prohibition, here it was in the beautiful healthy wholesome life on Roratonga. Indeed, everyone appeared charmed with the beauty, color, simplicity and happiness of this island. "By Jove! Roratonga is just what I wanted a South Sea Island to be!" was the felicitous way Mr. Radmore put it. Absolutely this charm would grow on one. It might not do to spend a long time at Roratonga. But I decided that some day I would risk coming for a month or two. We learned that at certain seasons fish were plentiful, especially the giant swordfish. Among the other islands of the Cook group was one over a hundred miles from Roratonga, rarely visited by whites, and said to be exquisitely beautiful and wonderful.

One of the passengers who boarded the *Makura* at Roratonga was Dr. Lambert, head of the Rockefeller Foundation in the South Seas. He was an exceedingly interesting man to meet. He had been eight years in the islands, and knew the native life as well as anyone living. He called Papeete an uncovered brothel; and indeed had no good word for any of the French islands. It was of no use, he claimed, to try to interest the French in improvements; and therefore he had not been able to let the Tahitians and Marquesans benefit by the splendid work being done by the Foundation.

Dr. Lambert clarified many obscure points in my mind. He was a keen close student, and he had been everywhere. Those writers who had recorded the havoc done by syphilis had simply been wrong. There is little or no syphilis in the South Seas. The disease, haws by name, has been mistaken for syphilis, but it is not a venereal disease.

Drink introduced by the traders has always been the curse. In those islands like Roratonga where the sale and trading of drink have been prohibited the natives have recovered their former happy and prosperous estate. Immorality among the young people remains about the same as it always has been, but the natives do not regard such relation as anything to be ashamed of. It is simple, natural, and has ever been so. The married woman, however, is usually virtuous.

On Tuesday, January thirteenth, we crossed the 180th meridian, and somewhere along there we were to drop a day, lose it entirely out of the week! I imagine that day should have been Tuesday, but the steamship company, no doubt for reasons of its own, made Saturday the day. How queer to go to bed Friday night and wake up Sunday morning! Where would the Saturday have flown? I resolved to put it down to the mysteries of latitude and longitude.

There was another thing quite as strange, yet wholly visible, and that was the retreat of the sun toward the north; imperceptibly at first, but surely! I saw the sun rise north of east and set north of west. As the *Makura* rushed tirelessly on her way, this northward trend of the sun became more noticeable. It quite changed my world; turned me upside down! How infinitely vast and appalling seem the earth and the sea! Yet they are but dots in the universe. Verily a traveler sees much to make him think.

PLATE VI

PLATE VII

PLATE VIII
GULLS AND SCHOOLS OF BAIT AT BIRD ROCK (Plates vi to xiii)

PLATE IX

PLATE X

PLATE XI

Plate XII

Plate XIII

CHAPTER III

THERE were two pearl traders on the *Makura* who had boarded the ship at Roratonga. One of them, Drury Low, had not been off his particular island for fifteen years. He was a strange low-voiced new type of man to me. I think he was Scotch. He lived at Aitutaki Island, one of the Cook group, said to be the loveliest island in the South Seas. His companion's name was McCloud. They gave me information concerning a great game fish around Aitutaki Island. They excited my curiosity to such extent that I got out photographs of yellow-fin tuna, broadbill swordfish, Marlin swordfish, and sailfish. To my amaze these men identified each, and assured me positively that these species were common in the Cook Islands. They also described to me what must be a sawfish, native to these waters. The yellow-fin tuna was called *varu* in the Cook Islands, *walu* in the Fijis, and grew to large size. Low saw one caught recently weighing one hundred and six pounds, and knew of others over a hundred. These were caught on hand-lines, trolling outside the reef. Recently a large one was hooked, and bitten in two by a shark. The smaller part that was hauled in weighed over two hundred.

The traders told of a Marlin being caught on a hand-line. It was a leaping fish, and over nine feet in length. McCloud then told of the capture of a sixteen-foot sail-fish, on a heavy hand-line. It took half a day to subdue this fish. A sixteen-foot sailfish, if at all heavy-bodied, would weigh at least five hundred, most likely more. I saw a picture of a fish that closely resembled the wahoo. They called it a kingfish.

To establish the fact of these great game fish in the South Seas was something of paramount importance to me, and the cause of much speculation. What might it not lead to? How incalculably are our lives influenced by apparently little things!

Never shall I forget my first absolutely certain sight of an albatross. It was on the afternoon of January fifteenth about two o'clock. I heard some one speaking of a wonderful bird following the ship, so I at once ran out. Wonderful bird? How futile are words! When I saw this sea bird of Ancient Mariner fame I just gasped, "Oh! Grand!" But then I have an unusual love for birds.

The albatross had a white body and brown wings that spread ten feet from tip to tip. They were a lighter color underneath. The breast, back and head were pure white; the body appeared to be as large as that of a goose; the head had something of an eagle shape, seen at such a distance. From head to tail there was a slight bow, sometimes seen in sea gulls. But it was the wing spread, the vast bow-shaped, marvelous wings that so fascinated me. I had watched condors, eagles, vultures, falcons, hawks, kites, frigate birds, terns, boobies, all the great performers of the air, but I doubted that I had ever seen the equal of the albatross. What sailing! What a swoop! What splendid poise and ease, and then incredible speed! The albatross would drop back a mile from the ship, and then all in a moment, it seemed, he had caught up again. I watched him through my glass. I devoured him. I yearned to see him close. How free, how glorious! I wondered if that bird had a soul such as Coleridge would endow him with. If dogs were almost human in their understanding of men, why could not wild birds have something as unusual? The albatross had always haunted me, inspired me, filled me with awe, reverence.

Late in the afternoon I espied another albatross, or at least one that on nearer view looked different. I climbed to the top deck and went aft to the stern rail, where I had an hour of delight in watching him from an unobstructed vantage point. The markings differed enough to convince me it might be another albatross. The body was flecked with brown, the neck ringed with the same color; the head like that of a frigate bird, only very much larger; the bill yellow, long and hooked. There was a dark marking on the white tail; the backs of the wings were dark brown, almost black, and the under side cream white except for black tips. He surely was a beautiful and majestic bird, lord of the sea. Where he swooped down from a height, he turned on his side so that one wing tip skimmed the waves and the other stood straight up. He sailed perpendicularly. He was ponderous, graceful, swift. A few motions of the wide wings sent him sailing, careening, swooping. He appeared tireless, as if the air was his native element, as no doubt it is, more than the sea. Once he alighted like a feather, keeping his large wings up, as if not to wet them. When he launched himself again it was to run on the water, like a shearwater, until he had acquired momentum enough to keep him up. Then he lifted himself clear.

Sunday morning at ten, January seventeenth, I sighted land. New Zealand! High pale cliffs rising to dark mountain ranges in the background swept along the western horizon as far as I could see.

While watching an albatross I was tremendously thrilled by the sight of an amazingly large broadbill swordfish. He was not over three hundred yards from the ship. His sickle fins stood up strikingly high, with the old rakish saber shape so wonderful to the sea angler. Tail and dorsal fins were fully ten feet apart. He was a monster. I yelled in my enthusiasm, and then ran for Captain Mitchell. But on my return I could not locate the fins. The fish had sounded or gone out of sight.

This was about fifteen miles offshore; and it was an event of importance. Swordfish do not travel alone.

Wellington, our port of debarkation, was a red-roofed city on hills surrounding a splendid bay. It had for me a distinctly foreign look, different from any city I had ever seen before; a clean cold tidy look, severe and substantial. From Wellington to Auckland was a long ride of fifteen hours, twelve of which were daylight. The country we traversed had been cut and burned over, and reminded me of the lumbered districts of Washington and Oregon. One snow-capped mountain, Tongariro, surrounded at the base by thick green forests, was really superb; and the active cone-shaped volcano, Ngauruhoe, held my gaze as long as I could see it. A thick column of white and yellow steam or smoke rose from the crater and rolled away with the clouds.

Auckland appeared to be a more pretentious city than the capital; and it likewise was built upon hills. It is New Zealand's hub of industry. From Auckland to Russell was another long day's ride, over partly devastated country and part sylvan, which sustains well the sheep and cattle of the stations thereabout. Farms and villages were numerous. The names of the latter were for me unpronounceable and unrememberable. They were all Maori names. At Opua, the terminus of the railroad, we took a boat for Russell. We were soon among picturesque islands above which the green mountains showed against the sky.

Russell turned out to be a beautiful little hamlet, the oldest in the island, and one with which were connected many historical events. The bay resembled that of Avalon, having a crescent-shaped beach and a line of quaint white houses. It is a summer resort, and children and bobbed-haired girls were much in evidence. The advent of the Z. G. outfit was apparently one of moment, to judge from the youngsters. They were disappointed in me, however, for they frankly confessed they had expected to see me in sombrero, chaps, spurs and guns. Young ladies of the village, too, were disappointed, for they had shared with people all over the world the illusion that the author Zane Grey was a woman. I found there in the stores, as at Wellington and Auckland, the English editions of my books.

Alma Baker, the English sportsman, arrived that night with his family, from Sydney, Australia. There were a number of Auckland anglers at the hotel. We were pleased to hear that several Marlin swordfish and two mako had already been taken at Cape Brett. The paramount interest of my trip, of course, was in the fishing; and I exhausted both anglers and boatmen with my curiosity and enthusiasm. Tackle, fish, methods, boats —everything was entirely new in all my experience. Salt-water angling was a development of only a few years there, and had not progressed far. It was plain that their rods, reels, etc., had been an evolution from the English salmon tackle. The rods were either a native wood called tanikaha or split cane with a steel center, and from seven to eight feet in length. The reels were mostly the large single-action Nottingham style from England, and were mounted on the under side of the rods. Guides and tips were huge affairs, and few and far between. Leaders, or "traces," as they were called, were heavy braided wire, twenty or thirty feet long, and the hooks were huge gangs, or three hooks in a triangle. The swivels were disproportionately small. Up to the year 1925 the anglers had used rod belts, but lately had developed swivel chairs with a fixed rod seat. They used a short heavy gaff, which was hooked round the tail of the fish, and if it was a shark he was harpooned in addition. The harpoon was really a crude heavy tozzle, mounted on a four-foot club. One of the New Zealand anglers brought out his tackle for our edification. Captain Mitchell and I surely handled it with thoughtful curiosity. We had to admit that these New Zealand anglers had performed some mighty achievements landing three, four and five hundred pound fish on such rigs. It looked like most of the energy exerted would be wasted.

Both anglers and boatmen explained their methods of fishing. They used dead and live bait. Trolling had been attempted at times, and persistently by some anglers, but it was never successful. Their best method appeared to be drifting with tide or wind, with live bait sunk ten or fifteen fathoms. One boatman told me he had caught twenty-four Marlin, three mako shark, and one thresher shark, most of which had been foul hooked, during the season of 1925. It was my opinion that this circumstance could be laid to the three-hook gang, and the drifting method. I was especially curious about this drifting with bait down deep, which was something I had always wanted to try on broadbill swordfish.

We were two days at Russell, part of which time was

taken up by a severe storm. When it cleared off the weather left nothing to be desired. Some one showed me a picture of New Bedford whaling ships at anchor in the bay. In the early days of whaling this place had been a favorite station for whalers, sometimes as many as thirty ships being anchored in the bay. What fishing days those must have been! Whaling had not entirely played out, and during our stay at Russell there was a small whaling steamer there. The captain had fished with the New Bedford and Nantucket whalers in those early days. He was most interesting. The season of 1925, just ended, had netted him some fifty-odd whales, mostly finbacks. What was of vastly more interest to me, he told of seeing schools of large round bullet-shaped fish lying on the surface offshore some fifteen or twenty miles. He said they had mackerel tails and silver bellies. That sounded decidedly like tuna. We were keen to learn more, but that was all the information available. The boatmen told of small tunny taken off Cape Brett. One of the scientific booklets on New Zealand fish mentioned long-fin albacore up to two hundred pounds caught by market fishermen. These were undoubtedly the Allison tuna. We listened to numerous stories about the hooking of great fish that never showed, and either broke away or had to be cut off after hours of fighting. Altogether the experiences and impressions of these anglers and boatmen proved the remarkable possibilities of a new and undeveloped fishing resort.

The boats reserved for Captain Mitchell and me were quite different from any we had ever used. They were close to forty feet in length, and eleven or twelve feet in beam. The cockpits were deep; so deep that we had to build platforms upon which to mount the fishing chairs we had brought from Avalon. It looked to us then that we would have our troubles fighting fish from these wide cockpits. On the other hand, the boats promised to be very seaworthy and comfortable. The *Marlin* was the widest boat, with rather high deck, and I decided it would be best for the motion-picture man and his equipment. The launch I was to use had the name *Alma G.*

We had to get permission from the New Zealand government to take these boats out of their district adjacent to Russell. The marine laws, and all laws, for that matter, were very rigid. Colonel Allan Bell and the Minister of Marine came to Russell to do all in their power to help make my visit to New Zealand waters a success. The Minister, at the earnest solicitation of Colonel Bell, finally agreed to allow us the privilege of taking our boats anywhere, but declared he would not grant that permission again. We were fortunate indeed.

Deep Water Cove Camp, about fifteen miles from Russell, was the rendezvous where anglers stayed while fishing the waters adjacent to Cape Brett. It accommodated ten or twelve anglers. I decided to follow my usual plan of being independent of everyone and having a camp of my own. We had brought our own tents, and we bought blankets. What wonderful blankets they were, and cheap! I never saw their equal. We outfitted at Russell, and soon were ready to start for Orupukupuku, an island belonging to Mr. Charles F. Baker, one of the leading citizens of the town, and said to be the most beautiful of all the hundred and more in the Bay of Islands.

As we ran down the bay, which afforded views of many of the islands, I decided that if Orupukupuku turned out to be any more striking than some we passed, it was indeed rarely beautiful. Such proved to be the case. It was large, irregular, with a range of golden grassy hills fringed by dark green thickets and copses, indented by many coves, and surrounded by channels of aquamarine

PLATE XIV

PLATE XV
SWORDFISH TOO CLOSE FOR COMFORT (Plates xiv to xix)

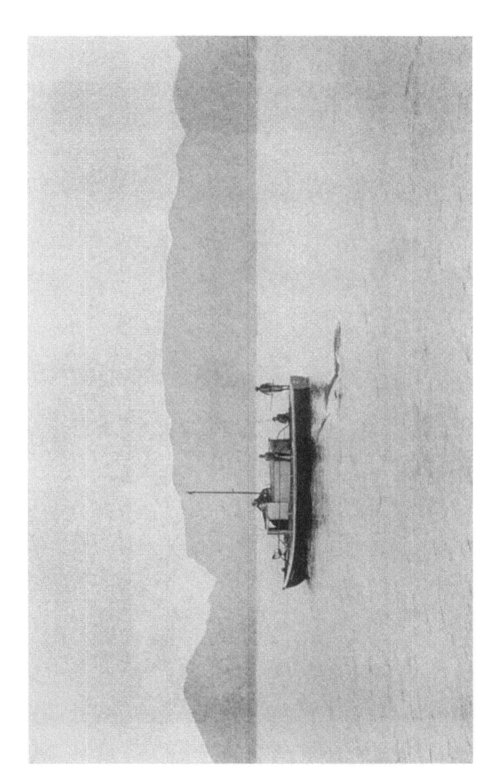

PLATE XVI

Plate xvii

Plate xviii

Plate xix

water, so clear that the white sand shone through. We entered the largest bay, one with a narrow opening protected by another island so that it was almost completely landlocked. The beach of golden sand and colored seashells stretched in graceful crescent shape. A soft rippling surge washed the strand, and multitudes of fish, some of them mullet, splashed and darkened the shallow waters. The hills came down to inclose a level valley green with grass and rushes, colorful with flags and reeds. A stream meandered across the wide space. On the right side were groves of crimson-flowering trees, the *pohutukawa*, in Maori. This tree was indeed magnificent, being thick, tall, widespreading, with massy clumps of dark-green foliage tipped by crimson blossoms. Beautiful as was this side of the bay, I decided to pitch camp on the other.

The hillside there was covered with a wonderful growth of the tree ferns, which plant has given New Zealand the name Fernland; a tall palmetto-like tree which the men called cabbage trees; and lastly tall marvelous *ti* trees. These stood up above close-woven thickets of the same flora. The foliage was very fine, lacy, dark green, somewhat resembling hemlock, and having a fragrance that I can describe only as being somewhat like cedar and pine mingled. How exquisitely strange and sweet! Trees and their beauty and fragrance have always been dear to me. The hills back of the bay were mostly bare, graceful, high, covered with long golden grass that waved in the wind.

These were my first impressions of our camp site on Orupukupuku. How inadequate they were! But first impressions always are lasting. These of mine I gathered were to grow.

When Mr. Alma Baker arrived, he pitched his camp under the crimson-flowered *pohutukawas* across from our place at the edge of the *ti* trees. We worked all day at this pleasant and never-wearying task of making a habitation in the wilderness. Never am I any happier than when so engaged. This nomad life is in the blood of all of us, though many comfort-loving people do not know it.

After dinner we climbed the high hill on our side. Fine-looking woolly sheep baa-ed at us and trotted away. The summit was a grassy ridge, and afforded a most extraordinary view of islands and channels and bays, the mainland with its distant purple ranges, and the far blue band of the sea. It was all so wonderful, and its striking feature was the difference from any other place I had ever seen. Seven thousand miles from California! What a long way to come, to camp out and to fish, and to invite my soul in strange environment! But it was worth the twenty-six days of continuous travel to get there. I gathered that I would not at once be able to grasp the details which made Orupukupuku such a contrast from other places I had seen. The very strangeness eluded me. The low sound of surf had a different note. The sun set in the wrong direction for me, because I could not grasp the points of the compass. Nevertheless, I was not slow to appreciate the beauty of the silver-edged clouds and the glory of golden blaze behind the purple ranges. Faint streaks or rays of blue, fan-shaped, spread to the zenith. Channels of green water meandered everywhere, and islands on all sides took on the hues of the changing sunset.

I was too tired to walk farther, so I sat down on the grassy hill, and watched and listened and felt. I saw several sailing hawks, some white gulls, and a great wide-winged gannet. Then I heard an exquisite bird song, but could not locate the bird. The song seemed to be a combination of mocking-bird melody, song-sparrow and the sweet wild plaintive note of the canyon swift. Presently I discovered I was listening to more than one bird, all singing the same beautiful song. Larks! I knew it before I looked up. After a while I located three specks in the sky. One was floating down, wings spread, without an effort, like a feather. It was a wonderful thing to see. Down, down he floated, faster and faster, bursting his throat all the while, until he dropped like a plummet to the ground, where his song ended. The others circled round higher and higher, singing riotously, until they had attained a certain height; then they poised, and began to waft downward, light as wisps of thistle-down on the air. I had never before seen larks of this species. They were imported birds, as indeed almost all New Zealand birds are. They were small in size. The color I could not discern. What gentle soft music! It was elevating, and I was reminded of Shakespeare's sonnet: "Hark! hark! The lark at heaven's gate sings."

They sang until after dark; and in the gray dawn, at four o'clock they awoke me from sound slumber. I knew then I had found a name for this strange new camp. Camp of the Larks!

CHAPTER IV

BOTH of my two boatmen were experienced at the New Zealand game of sea fishing. Arlidge was an engineer and Williams was a whaler. Both had been through the World War. In fact Captain Mitchell's two men had also had that experience. They could tell some yarns about that fight! Warne had been a cripple on the deck of a hospital ship which was torpedoed by the Germans. He was one of the few to be saved out of hundreds of sick and wounded soldiers. Those Germans left a record no civilization can ever forget! Evolution, the progress of mankind, the development of soul were left entirely out of their reckoning. How could they ever do anything but fail?

A circumstance related by one of the boatmen fascinated me. It was watching a torpedo come straight for the ship upon which he stood! like a graceful gliding fish with a white wake. How terrible it must have been to see!

Williams, the whaler, was a man nearing middle age, a brawny, powerful fellow who looked as if he could gaff and hold a heavy fish. And it certainly turned out that he could.

These men were all bewildered with my array of fishing tackle. They had never dreamed of such gear, and were tremendously interested. Like all good fishermen, they were boys at heart.

The second morning after our arrival in camp I was up before five. The tranquil bay, the burst of melody from the larks, the soft rose and pearl of the sky, the bleating of sheep from the hills—these and the many other details of my environment were exceedingly heart-satisfying. At six-thirty we were off toward the fishing grounds. Mr. Baker's boat had not arrived and he said he wanted to work around camp and overhaul his tackle. We ran among islands little and big, rocky and wooded, grassy and green, and on out the winding channel into the sea. Still we did not yet lose the land. A mountain range rose on our right, and terminated in Cape Brett, one of the great promontories of New Zealand. It was rugged and bold, showing the hard contact with wind and sea. A white lighthouse towered on the steep slope, a lonely sentinel, significant of the thoughtfulness of men.

We ran out to Bird Rock, which was a ragged black ledge rising a hundred feet or more above the thundering surge. This island was about even with the cape. Farther out was Piercy Island, a magnificent mountain of rock, begirt by a white wreath of foam.

Flocks of small white black-headed gulls were flying above a school of working fish that ruffled the water. Here and there were other patches, large as an acre. The place looked fishy, and here the boatmen began trolling with hand-lines for bait. They used a small gig, dark in color, shaped like a canoe, which they called a dummy. I rigged up a light tackle and put over a spoon, which the boatmen claimed would not be looked at by the *kahawai*. As luck would have it, however, I was the first to hook and land a *kahawai*. It was a lively fish, gray and green in color, shaped somewhat like a salmon. It had large scales. The mouth was small and delicate, which fact I soon saw accounted for the number of *kahawai* hooked and lost.

The fish were not biting well, so the boatmen ran out to Piercy Island, perhaps a matter of two miles. It towered just off the cape and was indeed an imposing spectacle. Black rock, green brush, wheeling gannets, white surf, roar and boom—all these thrilling things were old and familiar yet ever new.

When we ran under the looming shadow of this huge monument I laid aside my rod. That action was a considerable tribute for me to pay any place. I saw gray patches of fish on the surface, acres of *kahawai*. They all swam head out of the water, closely pressed together, and sending up little bursts of spray. Suddenly there was a white splash across the school, swift as light, and then a crash of water as thousands of *kahawai* leaped to escape some prowling enemy. This place did look fishy. My boatmen began to hook and haul away on *kahawai*, but they lost three fish to one they landed. The hooks were too small and sharp, and the men pulled too hard.

As we ran closer under the rock, near the line of black shadow, the water showed beautifully clear. There was not any perceptible swell in this protected lee. Riding the surface were hundreds of fish of varying hues, most striking of all being a wonderful cerise. Then there were purple fish, yellow fish, and gray *kahawai*, all scattered everywhere. The boatmen gave me the Maori names of these fish, but these names were so similar and so long and strange that I could not remember them. Besides, they surely were not the proper names. Fish and birds in different places usually have local names, but there is really only one correct name for any species. The boat-men called a shearwater, the kind I have seen all over the Pacific, a mutton bird.

Toward the end of Piercy Island a grand cave, the largest and highest I remember, ran through the rock in a tunnel fully a hundred yards long. It looked forbid-ding and dark, but it was really easy to run through. Even in the darkest part, where the water looked black, I saw the pale gleams of fish. On the outside, where the sea piled up on the cliffs, there was thunderous roar and heave of surge.

Practically all the fishing by anglers had been done near and around this rock. No anglers had ever run out to sea to any extent; and trolling, such as is the practice of American anglers, was practically unknown. The use of teasers behind the boat had never been heard of; and the fact of drawing Marlin swordfish up to the surface was quite incomprehensible to these boatmen.

We put over a couple of teasers and headed out to sea. The morning was fresh, cool, pleasant, with scarcely a ripple on the water. There was a slow swell running. We passed some shearwater ducks, and then a flock of large gannets. They looked like boobies to me, being large and long-winged, with yellow heads, bodies mostly pure white, and wings black-edged. We ran out four or five miles, until the shore line to the north showed rather low and dim. Cape Brett, however, loomed up black and clear, a reliable landmark for fishermen to watch.

We saw a big black fin, which even at a distance I knew to belong to a hammer-head shark. I did not have any particular yearning to catch him, but as sharks were counted by the New Zealand anglers and as I was in need of work, I dropped him a *kahawai*. He promptly took it, and I as promptly hooked him. I got about five minutes of work out of the loggy creature when he bit my line off; whereupon Captain Mitchell ran up, and seeing the shark surfacing again he handed him a bait.

Presently I had the pleasure of seeing the Captain hard at work with bent rod. I left him then and ran on out to sea. In an hour or more he caught up with my boat, and sure enough had the hammer-head on the stern. "Hooked him in the tail!" yelled the Captain; and I called back, "All right, Lucky Mitchell!" That sobriquet of Lucky I had once given to Frank Stick, and it surely was deserved; but as Stick was not in the Captain's class for luck I had to switch the honor.

We ran around outside for several hours without seeing any fish, and then headed back toward the cape. Presently I saw a swordfish jump, and I called out. The fish leaped three times. He was fully a mile away. We turned back and ran out at full speed. When we reached the place where I thought he had jumped we slowed down, and I began to troll a bait I had cut from a *kahawai*. My boatmen looked skeptical; but we had not completed our second circle when Arlidge let out a great yell and dived for the right teaser. Then I saw a big Marlin seize the teaser, break it off and throw it out. I let my bait back. He followed us, a wavering dark shape, coming closer, then dropping back, and again sheering toward us. I slacked off more line, and had a comfortable assurance this fish would bite. He was hungry, and he did bite, a good hard hungry tug. I let him run a hundred feet, and then struck. How those boatmen yelled! Captain Mitchell ran close. But the Marlin did not leap; he came up presently, made a swirl on the surface, and got free of the hook. I judged him to be a large Marlin, around three hundred pounds. The disappointment was keen, of course, but there was much satisfaction in having raised him by the teasers.

DOUBLE HEADER. TWO SWORDFISH HOOKED AT ONCE

PLATE XX

Embarrassing When They Go in Opposite Directions

PLATE XXI

After that we trolled around for a couple of hours without raising a fish; then we went in to the cape, where we found six other boats all fishing by the drifting method, and quite close together. I began to make observations with much curiosity and great interest. My boatmen caught a *kahawai*, hooked it through the back and dropped it overboard, letting out about seventy feet of line. Then we drifted. I did not feel that anything much would happen, so I contented myself with watching the other boats. I wondered about the long light rods, especially the native wood, tanikaha. Through my binoculars I could see anglers, rods, reels and lines quite distinctly. The tackle looked hopelessly inadequate, wholly miscast, as they say in motion pictures. But I was out to see and learn, and I was not preoccupied with my own ideas.

By and by somebody yelled, and we saw by the commotion on one of the boats that a fish of some kind had taken a bait. I waited. The boat was quite near. Finally the angler elevated his rod. How amazing to me that he did not strike! The rod bent a little, the line ran out, and the boatman headed his boat away from the scene of disturbance. Presently the fish came up, a Marlin of average size, and began what my boatmen called "breaching." That is the whaler's term for a whale breaking on the surface. This Marlin did not perform as do our California Marlin. He leaped about half out, and threshed on the surface while the boatman ran the boat away in the opposite direction.

"Now they'll lose that fish pronto," I soliloquized. And sure enough they did.

During the next two hours I saw two other swordfish lost in the same way. Another angler, fast to another fish, drifted away almost out of sight. I heard next day that he caught his, a small Marlin. Small in those waters meant one hundred and seventy-five pounds, as the smallest ever caught weighed one seventy-one.

Nothing happened to me. I was amazed to find after three hours that my *kahawai* was still alive and apparently little the worse for the brutal way in which he had been handled. I let him go and watched him swim away; then we ran back to camp.

It was indeed a pleasant camp to return to. We got back at six, when the sun was still above the hills, and the valley seemed full of golden lights and purple shadows. There was no wind; not a ripple on the bay. The larks were holding a concert. We had a supper that was most satisfying to me, after a week of traveling through cities and villages where I could not get the kind of home cooking I like. And that sunset! As I sat in camp, I felt that it was indeed good to be alive. My face felt warm from the heat of the sun. At dark we went to bed. When I looked out of my tent window I could see the Southern Cross and the Pointers that pointed to it. How strange and beautiful! This constellation of the southern hemisphere is more famous with mariners than the Dipper or other heavenly bodies, except perhaps Polaris.

I was up before sunrise. The grass held a thick coating of dew so thick my shoes were wet very quickly. The dew glistened from every blade and rush and leaf. The windless night accounted for such a precipitation.

At seven-thirty we were on the fishing ground near Bird Island, trolling for bait. Captain Mitchell had his teasers out, and suddenly he yelled and pointed! I looked in time to see a Marlin back of the left teaser. The Captain had no bait ready, so lost a good chance for a strike. Again we ran out to sea. There was quite a goodly swell and a ripple, making it fine for trolling. I expected results. We made for outside, and went fully twelve miles. I sighted two sunfish, recognizing them

[38]

easily by the peculiar side movement of the big fin. The other boat sighted a mako, but ran too close and put it down. On the return we traveled at quite a clip, too fast to troll, but I let out the teasers. From my place on deck I soon saw a waving purple fin, off to the starboard, and yelling to the boatmen I hurried aft; but I did not get to the teasers as quick as the swordfish. Four Marlin, one of them a monster, rushed the teasers; and two of them got hold. I pulled one teaser away while Arlidge pulled the other. Meanwhile Williams had dropped a *kahawai* overboard, with my hook in it; and as a Marlin rushed for it I grasped the rod hurriedly to get the tangled line clear. Just in time! The Marlin took that big six-pound bait, and went off with it. I was most curious. What would he do with it now he had it? Arlidge had thrown the clutch, and we drifted to a stop. The Marlin took a good deal of line. After a while I decided he had enough, so I struck him. I pulled the big bait away from him, just as I had imagined I would; but he came back after it, and that time I let him have it longer than I ever let even a broadbill play with a bait. Then I hooked him, coming up solid on a taut line. There was considerable excitement on my boat and on Captain Mitchell's.

The Marlin came out clear, showing himself to be one of the striped variety and around two hundred pounds in weight. Everybody got busy with cameras. He did not give us much of an exhibition, coming out only five times, and the last time not wholly out of the water. I brought him to the boat in sixteen minutes. He belonged to the same species as those we catch at Catalina. The little remoras, or sucking fish, were clinging to him, and dropped off as we hauled him astern.

We trolled about for two hours trying to raise another

or find the school we had raised, but were unsuccessful. Then we made for Piercy Rock.

I found the same boats there as we had seen the day before, all close together, all drifting with live bait overboard. I tried it again, and kept my eyes open. Some angler hooked a fish and went off to the north. The last I saw of him he was miles away. One of the boatmen on another boat called to us that his angler had fought a mako for two hours, and had lost it. During my first drift by the rock I saw one boat hook and lose a fish. Before I left another got fast and ran off with his quarry. Of course these anglers could not stop or hold a fish with the kind of tackle they used. I suppose they made it a process of exhaustion.

Next morning a launch visited our camp and reported that one of the Deep Water Cove anglers had fought a shark for eight hours. The head and tail were brought to us for identification. I called it a common sand or ground shark. It must have weighed over five hundred. I wondered how many of the heavy fish hooked at Cape Brett and never landed belonged to some such class. Probably most of them. Drifting with bait deep down could never be anything but shark fishing. At least most of the fish hooked would be sharks of some variety.

During our first two days' fishing we had raised six Marlin, one of which I caught. That looked favorable for trolling with teasers. This first Marlin weighed two hundred and twenty-six pounds, a long slim graceful fish. The largest of those we raised was twice the size of this one.

Late afternoon of the second day was calm and still— not a stir in the *ti* trees nor a ripple on the bay. The water reflected the rose-red trees and the golden hills, in an effect that seemed more like a fairy enchantment than mirrored sea and land. After supper I climbed the hill

FAST TO THE GREATEST FISH OF THE SEVEN SEAS—THE BROADBILL

PLATE XXII

First Broadbill Swordfish to be Caught on Rod in New Zealand
Waters

PLATE XXIII

to watch the sunset and the moonrise. The breathless stillness was something entirely new in my experience near the sea. No sound of surf! No moaning out on the bar! As the white moon soared above the hill the slopes and swales of grass took on a silver tint. I lingered to see and feel until I was so sleepy I could stay awake no longer.

Morning came, still, soft, rosy, balmy, colorful. Larks, up with the break of day, poured forth their perfect melodies. The grass was heavy with dew. Mullet and garfish were breaking the surface of the still water near the beach. Wide circles waved away and disappeared.

Beyond the bay the ocean, placid and smooth, resembled a mill pond. There was, however, a long low scarcely perceptible swell, which my watchful eyes detected. We ran out to the rocks for bait, and caught half a dozen *kahawai* in as many minutes. I saw a huge kingfish, so the boatman called it. He came up and lunged for a *kahawai* on the trolling line, making a sousing splash at the boat. If he was not a regular old yellowtail, belonging to the family *seriola*, then I missed my classification. The boatmen call this species kingfish; but kingfish belong to the mackerel family, and there was no mackerel about this fish. He looked to weigh close to a hundred, and made me keen to catch one.

Outside of Cape Brett we found the sea one vast glassy expanse. What a day to hunt for broadbill swordfish! I had not seen a better day in all my swordfishing at Catalina. Moreover, the air was pleasant, the shore line strikingly clear. I did not expect to see a broadbill swordfish, but I certainly could not help looking for one on such a sea as that. Birds were scarce. There was no sign of small fish on the surface. We ran out several miles, and all the while I perched on the deck, scanning the sea near and far. All at once I saw fins. I called out and stood up. We thought the fins belonged to a Marlin. Then we saw two more fish farther on, and formed the same conclusion about them. Suddenly the one nearest came up higher, showing his dorsal fin. I stared. I could not believe my eyes. Surely that brown-hooked rakish leathery dorsal could not belong to a broadbill swordfish, one of my old gladiator friends way down here in the Antipodes! But it did!

"Broadbill!" I yelled in wild excitement. "Look! . . . *Three broadbills!*"

Leaping for my tackle, I called for Arlidge to run around in front of the nearest fish. "Careful!" I warned. "Not too close!" At that he got close enough to scare a Catalina broadbill out of a year's growth, but the consequence was not so dire here. Williams threw out my hook baited with an eight-pound *kahawai* hooked through the back. I deplored that, but it was too late. I let out a hundred feet of line. The swordfish came on at my left, not quite an equal distance away. We glided ahead of him, and I dragged the bait fairly close to his path. Suddenly he saw it. He dove. I waited tensely. Indeed, the others on board were tense too. Nothing happened. I thought he had passed us by. Then he swirled up, showing half his bronze body, huge, glistening. I thrilled all over. He had lunged for the bait. I knew he would hit it, and so I called out. Did he hit it? Well, he nearly knocked the rod out of my hands. How that peculiar switching up of the line made me tremble! No other fish in the sea can give a line that motion.

The swordfish struck again, again, and the fourth time. It was great. I could scarcely realize the truth. Then he took the bait and made off slowly at first, then increasing his speed until he was going fast and my line was whizzing off the reel. When we had half of it off, two hundred and fifty yards, I shut down on the drag, and as R. C. would say, "handed it to him"!

In a moment more I knew I was hooked to a real old *Xiphias gladius*. He came up and showed his enormous shoulders, his high dorsal and half of his tail. Then he sounded.

The fight began, and as I wanted to excite these boatmen who had scarcely ever heard of a broadbill, I performed rather violently and strenuously, which soon told upon me. I got out of breath, and slacked up, until the fish ran out the line. He went down deep, which was disappointing, as I wanted him to do some surface stunts. He never showed again. In half an hour I was wet with sweat and thoroughly warmed up. I fought him hard. Long before the hour passed I knew I had on a very heavy swordfish. I could not do much with him, though sometimes it appeared I had the mastery. At the hour-and-three-quarters mark I shut down on the drag and let him pull. Here I found to my surprise that he could tow the boat. It was not a small boat, either. That, I knew, would be hard on him; and thereafter, when I needed a rest, I let him drag us a bit. Three-quarters of an hour of this sort of thing wore him out to the extent that I was soon getting line back and daring to hope for the best. He was so enormously heavy that I could not lift him more than a foot or so at each pump of the rod. He had been down a thousand feet. All this fight had taken place with the fish at a great depth, which was new in my experience. But every broadbill teaches you something new. Finally I was lifting this swordfish, beginning to feel assured that I might get him, when the hook began to rip. I felt it rip—rip—and come out! I reeled in the long line without saying a word. The boatmen felt the loss even more keenly than I. Yet I could not help deploring the usual manifestation of my exceedingly miserable luck as a fisherman; particularly in this instance, because the capture of the greatest game fish of all the Seven Seas here in the Bay of Islands waters of New Zealand would have meant much toward the development of the resort.

Later in the day I sighted a big Marlin fin on the surface of a swell; and that pleased me, for it proved that these New Zealand swordfish ride the swells the same as in other waters.

About three o'clock we ran in to the cape, and took to drifting, along with the other boats. Here again I rested while I was fishing (which was quite unique for me) and at the same time I kept close watch on the other boats, my glass bringing them right under my eyes. We let tide and wind take us at their will; and when we got half a mile or so off the rock we would run back and drift over again. During three of these drifts, of about an hour's duration each, I saw four boats lose fish, Marlin I was sure. One boat went out to sea with a fish, and I did not see what happened. Later we learned the angler of this boat caught his Marlin. I saw two anglers of another boat hook a fish on two rods. Despite this they ran off with the fish. Finally I got so curious to see the result that I had my boatmen follow. When we came upon the two anglers they had brought up a two-hundred-pound mako and at the moment were quite busily engaged. They had harpooned the fish. I saw the huge iron sticking out. The boatman was beating the mako over the head with a hammer, and another man was stabbing at the fish with what looked like a narrow spade. My conclusion was that the mako was not having a very happy time. He certainly had no opportunity to make what we anglers call a grand finish. This mako, the first I ever saw, and then did not have a good look at it, appeared to be a wild game fish. I grew more interested to catch one and see for myself what were its fighting qualities and its particular physical features.

As we ran back to camp the sky was overclouded, and the wind keen. It came off the land and threatened storm. By nightfall a strong breeze was blowing. If we had not been so well protected by hills we might have had to hold down our tents. At intervals during the night I awoke to thrill at the sound of the wind, strange in this far-away country. When I crawled out at dawn my first observation was that the grass was dry. Not a drop of dew! My second observation was that neither wind nor lowering sky affected the larks. What melody! There must have been half a dozen right around camp, singing to make me remember the beauty of the new day and the joy there is in life.

When we got outside of Piercy Rock that morning we found a choppy sea, and one most uncomfortable to fish. Captain Mitchell lagged behind for some reason or other, so I slowed down and waited. When he came up I found the reason was that he had caught a Marlin, his very first, a fair-sized fish. I whooped my congratulations, ending with, "Lucky Mitchell!"

We trolled that rough sea for several hours. No fins! No fish! Birds were plentiful, but wheeling around as if searching as hopelessly as we were. About eleven o'clock we ran in behind Piercy Rock. Seven other boats were there drifting. Schools of *kahawai* were shining on the surface, and flocks of gulls hovered near, sometimes alighting on the water, in the thick of the schools, evidently feeding on the tiny minnows the *kahawai* were chasing. The surge against the beetling cliffs was magnificent. Roar and crash and boom! Then a white cascade came pouring down from the bronze slant of rock, to disappear in the great gulf left by the receding swell.

Soon the surge heaved in again, to swell and grow and mount high, and go crashing to ruin. Restless and eternal sea! How it chafed the rocks! Those great cliffs really looked impervious to the contending tide; but a second glance showed that the sea was wearing away the rock and in time, in the ages to come, would conquer.

One boatman passing us called to Williams that he had lost a Marlin. So this made eight or nine I had recorded in three days, out of eleven hooked.

By the time we had completed our first drift I had developed conclusions. I knew that Marlin or some other large fish were working along with the schools of *kahawai*, every now and then making a charge from underneath, which caused the *kahawai* to leap crashing on the surface. So I instructed my boatmen to keep near one of these schools, and I let my bait drift as close as possible. This was something I had not observed a single one of the other boats doing, yet it seemed the thing to do. Soon I had a strong pull on my line. My bait was ten times too large, and the hook was also large, at least for Marlin. So when I struck, it did not surprise me to miss. I slacked the bait back, and sure enough the Marlin took it again. This time I let him have it so long that he came up on the surface and ejected it. But he got tangled up in my line, whereupon began a pretty exhibition. I was afraid to pull hard for fear of cutting my line. The fish leaped and threshed and came at the boat. In the vernacular of the boatmen, he breached twenty-five times. By handling him gently I saved both fish and line. When we got him fast we discovered my hook and bait were over a hundred feet from the place on my line where the Marlin had tangled.

We ran back and caught another *kahawai*. While beginning another drift one of the other anglers hooked a fish and started out to sea. It sort of aggravated me to watch these boats run away with a fish.

Presently I saw another patch of *kahawai* acting suspiciously, so I stalked it, and soon had another strike. This fish was easy to hook; and as there were eight boats near by I exerted myself in my desire to have them see a rod bent. The result was that I brought this Marlin up in eleven minutes. He did not jump, which was due to his being badly hooked. Running back to the rock, I tried again, found another school of *kahawai* on the surface, and had another heavy strike. But this fish let go quickly. He must have felt the hook. Thereupon I called it a day and left for camp. Captain Mitchell's fish weighed one hundred and ninety-two pounds, and mine two hundred and fifty-two and two hundred and eighty-four, respectively. The larger fish was a fine specimen that I had judged to be around three hundred pounds in weight.

Though the late afternoon was stormy, all the boatmen went to Russell to see their families, and no doubt to talk fish, especially the broadbill battle. I could not very well quote some of their exaggerations, though the temptation is strong. But all of them had come out frankly in expressing their amazement and admiration and to indorse heartily our tackle and method.

Some of the anglers we had watched, and boatmen too, apparently did not know how to proceed when a fish took hold of their bait. I saw one instance that is worth recording, since it was both funny and tragic. Four men were in a boat near us. Manifestly a bite had been felt by one of them, for they all jumped up. The man with the rod held it up high, but he did nothing else. I saw the long tip bend and then nod. Evidently the line was paying off the reel. Promptly a fine big swordfish broke water several hundred feet astern. Then great excitement prevailed. All the men, except the angler with the rod, ran around in that boat. The engineer started the boat at full speed, slowed down, turned around, went fast again, and finally got the swordfish on the other side of the boat. I did not know what had happened to the angler, but I saw him leap up, trying to hold the long rod. It jerked down, bent to the water and then under the boat. In an instant more it sprang back straight. The angler stood bewildered, while one of his comrades began to thread the broken line through the guides. All this happened in a half a minute or so. After it had happened they all sat down, probably for a conference. I wanted much to run over there and give them some instructions, but I managed to refrain.

My largest swordfish, two hundred and eighty-four pounds, had four fish in his gullet, two *kahawai*, a small blue shark, and a snapper fully seven pounds in weight. This last had a round hole straight through his body. Unquestionably, it had been made by the bill of the swordfish. The snapper had not been struck a side blow in the usual way Marlin kill or stun their prey; he had been rammed straight through. This was proof that the spearfish, or Marlin, can and do ram fish. No doubt they ram their enemies in battle, as the broadbills do.

An incident of the day that pleased me immensely was to run across a market-fishing boat manned by two sturdy dark-faced fishermen; a sloop, scarred by sea and weather, and with the name *Desert Gold* on the stern. We ascertained that it had been named after my book *Desert Gold*, the same as had one of the greatest race-horses ever bred in the Antipodes. I was touched, proud, tremendously pleased. I had met with innumerable instances of kindly recognition from my

End of a Perfect Day

PLATE XXIV

SPEEDING CAMPWARD

PLATE XXV

reading public in the Antipodes, but to discover an old sailboat, under the beetling brow of Cape Brett, named with one of my own book titles, was something singularly affecting to me. Those fishermen never guessed the true state of my feelings.

CHAPTER V

THE boatmen told me this story about a mako fight that seems incredible. Yet they staked their word on it, and offered confirmation from others. A mako took a *kahawai*, was hooked and fought awhile. He tore free from the hook, and in plain sight took another bait thrown to him. Then the battle went on again for an hour or more, when he broke the line. He came up near the boat. They threw him another *kahawai* and he took that. This time the tackle held and he was landed, a fish of over three hundred pounds.

I have heard some fish stories in my day, and this one ranks high. But I believe it. I have known as strange facts myself, really stranger than any homespun fabrications. The most bewilderingly preposterous and stunning fish stories sometimes are true.

On the afternoon of our fourth day the threatening weather developed into a storm. Next day we found a rough sea and squalls of rain, but we persevered for a while. Captain Mitchell hooked some kind of a heavy beast, as he called it, that soon got away; and later he raised a big kingfish to the teasers. This was the third he had brought up. I had no luck whatever, and about noon, when the wind increased to a gale, I ran in, and the Captain soon followed.

On and off it rained and blew all the afternoon. We had trouble holding down the tents until they got thoroughly wet. During the night, at intervals, the storm awoke me. The sound of surf, the wind in the *ti* trees, the patter of rain, all were singularly pleasant. By morning the storm had passed and the larks were proclaiming the fact with joy.

The promise of a fine day was not fulfilled, however, and outside the islands the sea was lumpy, bumpy, humpy, and reflected leaden clouds. At rare intervals the sun came out, the sea turned blue, and there seemed to be some sense in fishing. These intervals, however, were few and far between. I was in for a hard day. Many, many of them have I had. The way to fish is to keep your bait in the water, and keep on going, or casting, or sitting still on a log, whatever the particular method of the hour, until you get a bite.

The *Alma G.*, though the best craft in Russell, was an uncomfortable boat. Her motions were sudden. She was a cross between a V bottom and a round bottom. I had to hold on to my seat, hour after hour, and to my rod also. I trolled until one o'clock without sign of fish or strike. Then I climbed on deck to look for birds or anything. We were miles out. Gradually we worked back toward the cape.

At last we reached the shelter of Piercy Island. Four boats were drifting on the lee side of the great rock. We caught a live *kahawai* and began to fish. The sun shone now and then, the wind blew a gale about as often. Two more hours passed, negative for me. No, not altogether that, for the smallest and prettiest gull I ever

saw alighted on my boat, quite close to me, and regarded me with bright friendly eyes. He had fluffy
feathers, like spindrift, white as snow with a few specks
of black. Presently he walked aft and perched upon
the deck. Next, a bird I classified as a sooty shearwater
swam up to us. He too was small and round, but precisely the hue of soot. The boatmen fed him bits of fish
and then Williams reached down, picked him up and set
him on the combing. I was amazed and delighted. New
Zealand birds were indeed tame. This one looked in-
sulted at having his feathers ruffled, but he did not show
any fright.

Upon turning the corner of Piercy Rock I discovered
Captain Mitchell frantically engaged with a Marlin
swordfish that was running and jumping toward the cliff.
I hurried to get my camera. When I came out with it I
was just in time to see the swordfish make a long high
leap that ended against the stone wall. He splintered
his spear, which I saw fly into bits. He ejected the
bait and also the hook. Then hanging there in a niche, he
floundered and beat and flapped until he slid back into
the surge.

There did not appear to be any lee side to the island,
as the wind whipped round all sides, and increased in
strength until nothing could keep its place in the boat,
nor I safely hold my chair. So we beat back to camp.

When Captain Mitchell returned he expressed himself forcibly: "Rotten day! I saw four Marlin, and had
two strikes. The second one after you left. We saw
a big Marlin on the surface, and we ran ahead of him
with a bait. He took it and swam off in plain sight, trying to get it in his mouth. I let him go with it. Then
when I struck the hook didn't catch. The Marlin took
the bait again, and though I let him have it a long time
I couldn't hook him. Those *kahawai* are too big.

CAPTAIN MITCHELL'S 367-POUND STRIPED MARLIN

PLATE XXVI

WEIGHING SWORDFISH

PLATE XXVII

They're a darned nuisance. There was a splendid fish,
hungry as a wolf, and I missed him!"

" 'Right-o,' as these boatmen say," I replied. "This
kahawai bait is too large for anything but sharks. It is
the wrong bait for swordfish. And this method of drifting is wrong. We've got to find a suitable bait and a
better method. Weather permitting, we can troll, of
course."

The situation indeed presented some perplexities. I
was satisfied that the waters along the New Zealand
coast were alive with these great game fish, and no doubt
fish that were new and equally formidable. We had discovered in calm weather we could find broadbill and also
raise Marlin. These facts were significant and inspiring.
But the whole job was a pioneering one and must take
time, hard work and infinite patience.

That night I surely did not see the stars. With sky
pitch-black, and strong southwest winds, it appeared the
storm was not over. Morning broke calm, however, with
rosy sky and placid bay; and we were in high hopes again.
Yet by the time we got out to Cape Brett the sky had
grown overcast, the sea ruffled and white. Behind the
huge castle-like island there was a lee of considerable
extent, where we proposed to fish a little despite the
storm. Gale and sea grew more violent. The mainland was lost in a haze of rain. Around the yellow cliffs
the surges rose grandly and burst with sullen boom.
What a cork at the mercy of the sea seemed our boat!
I began to try to convince myself that we should run
in before the storm increased, and just then I saw a
Marlin fin.

We followed him, trolling a bait, got ahead of him,
and had the fun and excitement of seeing him swerve
swiftly and flash green as he seized it. The other boat
drew near. My Marlin swam on with the big bait

[53]

plainly visible between his jaws. Captain Mitchell thought the swordfish had passed my bait, and tried to give him his. It took some yelling to show the Captain his error. Finally some one in his boat saw the swordfish with my bait. At last I grew impatient, and jerked the bait away from that nonchalant beggar; then he rushed it.

I hooked the Marlin before he had time to swallow the bait, with a result I expected. He leaped. He plunged. He rose half out of the water and plowed over the sea directly at Captain Mitchell's boat. Those on board had some chances with cameras at close range, for my swordfish came out twenty-three times. After that he sounded. Then in rather short order I brought him in.

When we reached Piercy Rock again there were four other boats about, one of them Mr. Alma Baker's with Sid, the boatman of local fame. The sun was shining and the wind had abated, all happening in such very short order that I thought after all the day might turn out well.

As soon as we secured another bait Arlidge sighted a mako. We trolled the bait in front of him. He shot under; and in another moment I felt a strong tug, then a run. When I struck I waited breathlessly to see the mako leap, but he did not. I found him fast and powerful. Nevertheless, I soon had him in for Williams to gaff. Then pretty quickly I learned something about mako! He put up a terrific battle, broke one gaff, soaked us through with water, and gave no end of trouble. The boatmen wanted to harpoon him, but this I would not allow. Such a game fish should be given the same sporting chance afforded to others. Eventually we subdued the mako and hauled him aboard, to find ourselves two miles out to sea.

That was the beginning of a day too full to be wholly recorded. The wind ceased, then blew hard again; the sun shone, then became obscured by clouds; the sea was both rough and smooth.

One of the Deep Water Cove anglers hooked a fish quite near us. I watched. Suddenly a blue-and-white fish shot into the air, high, higher, as if propelled by a catapult.

"Mako! Mako!" the boatmen yelled.

The mako turned over, cut the water like a knife and went out of sight; then leaped again, this time still more wonderfully. Down he went slick, like a champion diver. Up again, high—fully thirty feet! I shouted in my excitement. He turned clear over in the air, and slid down into the sea. He did not show again.

"Well, that mako is some fish!" I ejaculated. And the boatmen were loud in their praise of what they consider their gamest fish.

During the next hour I saw three boats hooked to fish, all at the same time. Alma Baker's fish took him out to sea.

I saw another angler break one of the long limber rods. Captain Mitchell broke a line on another fish. We saw half a dozen Marlin tails during the afternoon. I got a bait in front of one fish. He charged it, but refused to bite. Three times he did this. He was pugnacious but not hungry. These Marlin had fed, and were on their way out to sea, which is their habit in all waters.

It took the angler three hours to land his mako. During that time several other anglers lost fish. Captain Mitchell had a Marlin get fast in a loop of his leader, and pull free at the boat.

About four o'clock I had a tremendous strike. When I hooked the fish Williams had a strike on my other rod, which he was holding. We thought there were two fish.

But after half an hour of hard work we found I had hooked the Marlin, and Williams had got it tangled in his leader.

Not counting three I landed, I saw ten fish hooked, and of these three brought in. My Marlin weighed two hundred and fifty-four and two hundred and eighty-five pounds, respectively, and the mako two hundred and fifty-eight.

It did not take more than one quick glance at my mako, when I saw him out of the water, to pronounce him a remarkable, a terrible, and even a beautiful fish.

No doubt ichthyologists would relegate him to the shark family, and I was compelled to do that also, but I never saw a shark before with any of this one's marked features. He actually had something of the look of a broadbill swordfish without the sword. Dark on the back, white underneath, round and massive of body clear down to the tail, with the flattened side protuberances very marked, thick to the juncture with the flukes, he indeed gave a first impression of being some relation to old *Xiphias gladius*.

It was in the head and tail that he differed so essentially from a broadbill, or any other kind of fish. The head resembled a bullet, coming to a sharp point, long and slim. The eyes were large, protruding, and most singularly harmonious, with the huge jaw set far back and armed with the most formidable array of teeth nature could devise. They were long, crooked, white, sharp as needles, and many of them set irregularly. In life these teeth had the physical property of moving to and fro, like the teeth of a reaper. The boatmen claimed that when the mako lost a tooth he developed a new one very quickly, and that he had rows of them in reserve in the jaws.

The tail was a beautiful thing, spade-like, only curved,

graceful, symmetrical. The upper lobe was larger, with a tiny notch on the upper outside; the lower lobe almost oval in shape, as were the dorsal fins. The pectoral fins were long, wide, massive.

Here was a sea creature, an engine of destruction, developed to the nth degree. I had never seen its like. Even an orca could not do any more ravaging among sea fish. Every line of this mako showed speed and power to a remarkable degree. He had five long deep gill slits on each side of his neck. I was amazed and fascinated by this new fish. Mr. Morton, a New Zealander, who accompanied us as a motion-picture camera man, explained how the Maoris used to capture the mako, the teeth of which they prized most highly. The Indians took spears, a rope, and a very long pole, and went in a canoe to places known to them to be infested with mako. A sting ray or skate was fastened on the end of the long pole, and then was thrust down into the water, in and out, until it had excited a mako. When they had teased the mako up to the canoe, which was easy, for this fish does not fear man, they manipulated the skate so that the mako in rolling over and turning for it would give the Maoris a chance to throw a noose over its tail. With this fast to the fish they had a swift and precarious ride. When they wanted to turn the canoe they got in the center. The weight all at one point in the center caused these Indian canoes to swerve. They would seldom upset. By such dexterous means the Maoris tired out the mako and dispatched it with spears. I could not help but contrast their courage and enterprise with the Indians along the Mexican coast, who were afraid to venture out on the sea.

The fourth day of the blow was the worst of all. Still we went fishing. As before, there was a lee on the sea side of the islands. It was not so large as the day pre-

vious, nor so smooth, but we managed to make some kind
of shift at fishing. We surely did drift. There were
seven boats altogether. I was the first to raise a Marlin,
a fine fish, that ran all over the place, leaping and smashing the water, and making us follow him out into the
rough sea. I had all I wanted for three-quarters of an
hour. The big swells made fighting the fish a most difficult and laborsome task.

In the afternoon Captain Mitchell hooked a heavy fish
of some kind. I was near enough to ascertain that. His
boatmen began to run away from the fish. I hurried out
there, and found they were doing as I had seen most of
these New Zealand boatmen, who, the minute a fish was
hooked, would run the boat after it. The anglers do not
get any chance to fight a fish, in instances of this kind. I
shouted for the Captain's men to throw out the clutch.
With the boat stopped Mitchell got down to determined
work on the fish, and it soon showed on the surface, a
mako. We ran closer in the interest of picture-taking.
But I was to find that photographing a mako had its difficulties. It did not seem possible to keep track of the fish.
I heard the boatmen yell, and a second later the crashing
plop of the mako as he fell back from his leap. But I did
not see it. Some time after that he jumped again, too
quickly for me to focus upon him. What a clear swift
powerful leaper!

Captain Mitchell whipped his mako, after a good hard
battle in a bad sea. The fish had chewed off one of our
best wire leaders, and would certainly have escaped but
for a loop of the leader being round his tail.

We ran back to discover two other boats engaged on
fish of some kind. Alma Baker was one of them. Upon
going close to him I found he had a long slim ugly blue-
colored shark which his boatman was holding by the
leader. I took a picture. I had to bite my tongue to keep

[58]

from yelling to that boatman, for I knew he would break the brute off; and he did.

During the rest of the afternoon there were indications of a change in the weather, which we certainly welcomed. Upon arriving at camp we weighed our fish. My Marlin tipped the scales at two hundred and seventy-six, the Captain's mako at two hundred and ninety-four. The leader was a sight to behold, and caused me much concern. We had prepared especial thirty-foot mako leaders, heavy wire that we had believed was indestructible. What would we do if we hooked some really big mako?

The wind kept deceiving us, veering and lulling, blowing a gale at night, falling in the morning, and then rising again. It made heavy seas. On February fourth I lost two fish, one a hammer-head that first bit my bait in two, then came back for the second portion. He was cunning and I was rather careless. There is never any excuse for not hooking a hungry shark. In this case I did not wait long enough, so that when I struck the hook did not hold. My second misfortune was on a Marlin of goodly size, that I worked too strenuously, and the hook pulled out as I brought him into the boat.

The next day was fine and promising at dawn, but the sun and calm were only delusions. A northwester sprang up, and blew harder every minute. There were seven boats out and they had a sorry time of it. Nevertheless I had a wonderful strike from a Marlin that shot by the boat and came out in a beautiful leap before I had time to hook him, but the hook held. We had to chase this fellow out into the rough sea, where I had another hard battle with fish and swells combined. He took us a mile off Piercy Rock. One other boat got fast to a Marlin, and went out to sea so far that we lost sight of it altogether. Pretty risky in a small boat! I asked my men how these fellows would communicate their difficulties if the boat broke down or they ran short of gasoline. They said there would be no way. No accidents had happened at this new fishing resort, so the serious side of the game had not received any consideration.

The gale increased, and I thought it best to run in. Before we got far I was indeed glad I had started. The sea was running "high, wide and handsome," as the cowboys sometimes call the bucking of a mean bronco. The *Alma G.* proved a seaworthy craft and gave me confidence. Her bow was under water a good deal of the time, and she became as wet as a duck in the rain. When we got in the green shallow water the swells ran tremendously high and swift. They lifted us and sped us forward, so that with the added celerity we were indeed racing. Exhilarating and thrilling as that was, I was glad to run in between the first islands to smooth water. My Marlin was a superb specimen of two hundred and sixty-eight pounds, long, slim, brilliantly striped, and with a very long spear. If he had been fat he would have weighed far over three hundred.

About supper time a heavy squall swooped down into the bay. We had to exert ourselves hurriedly and strenuously to keep our camp from blowing away. Both the launches dragged their anchors and grounded on the bar at low tide, wherefore the boatmen were most actively engaged during the gale and a downpour of rain. For me it was all fun. To be out in a rainstorm always takes me back to boyhood days.

About sunset the clouds broke up into irregular masses, the gale subsided, patches of vivid blue sky shone through rifts, and an exquisite light, as if the air were full of dissolved rainbows, began to be manifest on all sides.

The phenomenon lured me to climb the high slope and wade through the wet grass to the summit, where I could face the glorious west. Rain blew in my face, a cool misty rain that did not obscure my sight, though evidently it had remarkable effect upon the atmosphere. A strange transparent medium enveloped earth and sky. The sun had set below a strip of dark cloud. Behind that the intense blue sky reached to broken cumulous clouds, purple in mass, edged with silver, shot through with rays of gold. From this great flare of the west spread the beautiful light over range and islands, bays and hills. The slopes with their waving grass were crowned by an amber glow; the bay on the leeward side of the island was a deep dark green; that on the windward side a white-ridged purple. From over the far hill thundered the turbulent sea. To the south the mountains showed dimly through the pall of storm that had passed over the Bay of Islands. The whole panorama seemed to possess an unearthly beauty, delicate, ephemeral, veiled by some mysterious light.

To make the moment perfect there were larks above my head singing as if the magic of that sunset inspired their song. My searching gaze located three—one near, scarcely a hundred feet above me; another quite far; and a third a mere speck in the sky. There were others I could not find. Those I watched poised fluttering on high, singing such a sweet plaintive song as surely never equaled by other bird, both in melody and in meaning. They were singing in the rain; and to my intense astonishment I ascertained, quickly in case of the nearer larks and after hard peering at the third, that they had their heads pointed to the west. This might have been accident; but I was not one who could deem it so. Nor were they singing for any other reason save the joy of life! I watched them until they dropped, wafted straight down, to cease their songs as they neared the ground. Two of them alighted in the wet grass and did not arise; the third dropped out of sight behind the hill. Others were near, invisible, but wonderfully manifest by their music.

Darkness gradually gathered in the valleys of the island, and twilight fell upon the hill. The glory died out of the west, the intensity of color away from islands and bays. Rain still fell, mistily, cool, sweet to the face. When I reached the foot of the slope larks were still singing somewhere.

All experience must be measured as much by what one brings to it as by what it gives. Grassy windy hilltops, above the sea or the valley, always have enthralled me. They must surely have had strange relation to the lives of some of my ancestors. This experience on a hilltop of Orupukupuku, in the Bay of Islands, seemed fraught with unusual appreciation of nature and clearness of the meaning of life. My fishing was the merest of incidentals. It must be a means to an end, or one aspect of an end. How many times, on some adventure in a wild country, or some fishing jaunt to new waters, have I been rewarded by a singular revivifying joy, similar to this I found on the wet grassy top of Orupukupuku, the rich amber light filling my eyes, and the songs of the larks in my ears!

CHAPTER VI

THE government weather authorities of Auckland gave out the information that the gale we had been experiencing was owing to violent disturbances in the Antarctic. Personally, it was my first conviction that the upset of the sea occurred at Cape Brett, and right under my boat. I have attempted to fish some rough waters in my day, but this maelstrom around Piercy Rock had the distinction of being the worst. There was, however, one consolation—it beat the rough water of the Gulf Stream at Long Key, Florida, by a goodly margin. I had imagined the northeast trade-wind of the Gulf to be about the worst!

Captain Mitchell and I took the Radmores out, one in each boat; and needless to say we fervently prayed for the gale to lull or that the Radmores would react naturally and suggest we return to camp. But these English brothers had not only served in the British Royal Navy; they had traveled in ships all over the globe. The elder Radmore, who accompanied me, appeared to enjoy the spindrift flying off the waves into our faces, and the pitching of the boat bow first, and the rocking counter motion from side to side like a cradle. There were seven other boats out, manned by anglers and boatmen apparently as crazy to fish as we were. Six hours of stinging wind, of scudding spray, of tossing seas, of dangerous ventures near the rocks trying to find calm water where there was none, of futile fishing and of most annoying and increasing discomfort, were added to my angling experience that February day. This was the eighth day of adverse winds and crisscross seas.

The following day we did not trust, for it dawned precisely like the one before, and a gentle breeze soon developed volume and power, and the low bank of gray cloud in the southwest soon overcast the sky. Yet at intervals the wind lulled and the sun shone warm. There were promises of better weather in a more or less remote future.

Hours in camp, however, were not wasted or idled. There were manifold tasks, including notes, tackle, photography, letters and exploring the many ramifications of the beautiful Orupukupuku Island. Though not a pretty comparison, to liken the island to the shape of an octopus was not too far-fetched. It had at least a dozen rambling arms, projecting out into the bay, as if to point toward the other islands. Some of them were a long way from camp, over grassy hills and down grassy canyons, and then out on waving undulating grassy ridges to promontories overlooking the sea.

There was one lonesome horse on the island, and I appeared always to encounter him on my walks. He regarded me with most evident surprise and concern; and he either was really wild or wanted me to think so. I observed, however, that as these meetings increased in number he grew less inclined to kick up his heels and go galloping off with flying tail and mane.

The locusts that sang their summer songs during the day were hard to locate in the *ti* trees. At length, however, I got a glimpse of one, and he appeared black in color and rather small in size. Huge flies were present in considerable numbers, always buzzing and humming around when the wind lulled and the sun came out. They were not otherwise annoying.

We had a glimpse of quail in the reeds of the swale back of camp. I saw what I believed to be a swamp blackbird. In the dense grove of trees behind our tents there were sweet-voiced birds, so shy and illusive that I could not discover what they looked like. Then on a low level slope I flushed a skylark out of the grass. It flitted and flapped over the grass as if it had a broken wing, after the deceiving habit of a ruffed grouse when driven from her nest. This lark had answered to the same instinct, to lure the intruder away from her little ones. I soon found the tiny nest deep-seated in a tuft of grass, and surely safe from anything except the sharp hoof of a sheep. There were three young birds, not long hatched, with scarcely a feather. I slipped away to a knoll and watched for the mother bird to return; but evidently she saw me, for she did not come.

When we hauled a fish up on the beach, to weigh and photograph, there were always a number of large black-winged gulls that appeared so suddenly as to make me suspect they had been watching. They might have been attracted by scent. At any rate they arrived and they were hungry. In the mornings, at daylight, I would hear them screaming on the beach, their notes at once piercing and musical. These gulls, by the way, were differently marked from any other I had observed.

Captain Mitchell related an adventure which I genuinely envied him. A giant albatross darted down behind his boat, while he was trolling a *kahawai*, and dived at

[65]

the bait, tugged hard, then let go. Seen at close range the bird appeared enormous, austere and old, gray and white with black markings. He had a spread of wings that was incredible. The Captain let his bait drift back, in hopes that the albatross would take it and hook himself. What a catch that would have been! But the weird fowl of Ancient Mariner fame was not to be captured. Ponderously, yet with the grace of a swallow, he swooped down and circled once more over the bait, then sailed away with the flight so marvelous and beautiful to see.

Before sunrise the next morning I was up strolling along the beach, where I had been lured by the still soft dawn. No wind to speak of! It was a change vastly to my liking. At low tide the sandy crescent beach was fully a hundred yards wide and thickly strewn with shells. One of my myriad pastimes is gathering shells cast up by the sea.

This morning, however, my attention was distracted from my pleasant search by a crash in the water. I looked up in time to see one of the large white-and-black gannets fly right out of the water. The depth there could scarcely have exceeded a foot. Multitudes of little fish were leaping on all sides of the violent place from which the gannet had emerged. Most assuredly he had dived among them for his breakfast. I wondered how he could plunge down into that shallow water without killing himself on the sand.

Whereupon I watched him as he sailed away along shore, circling out around the boats, to turn back toward me. He was flying some forty or fifty feet above the water. About opposite my position mullet were breaking on the surface. No doubt that the gannet saw them! Suddenly he swooped down until he was scarcely two feet above the water. Then he bowed his wings and dived; quite the slickest dive imaginable! His white body gleamed under the water and must have covered a distance of six feet. Then he came up just as suddenly and in his cruel bill was a luckless little fish, which he swallowed kicking.

"I doff my hat to you, Mr. Gannet," I said admiringly, and indeed I suited action to words.

There is never any end to the marvelous things to be seen in nature. Always new, strange and wonderful things, not always beautiful! Self-preservation is the first law of nature, but it is a hard bloody business.

Too good to be true—the change in the weather! The breeze was soft, and clouds were few. We made skeptical remarks about how the wind would come up, gather strength and blow the tops off the waves; but it did not. All day the conditions improved. The gusts grew shorter of duration and farther apart. Warmer shone the sun. The sea gave evidence of calming down. It was enough for me to sit in my boat and be grateful for these welcome facts, and smell the fragrant wood smoke that came from forest fires on the hills.

Twelve boats drifted around Piercy Rock that morning. We saw two Marlin fins the very first thing, before we had caught a bait. After we did catch one we could not locate the Marlin. During the morning two fish were hooked outside the rock, one of which, a small swordfish, I saw landed.

After lunch I had a strike. When hooked the fish ran three hundred yards as swiftly as an express train. Then plunging out, he turned straight back, with like speed. His dorsal fin cut the water for a hundred feet. Then I lost him. My line went slack. We thought he had broken off, with all the bag of line he was dragging. I wound in my line up to the double before I felt him right at the boat.

Then he began to leap, and by the time he had ended his beautiful and remarkable exhibition of pyrotechnics he had come into the air fifty times. He made every manner of leap except a somersault. The boatmen used up all the films on both my cameras. That tremendous burst of energy had exhausted the swordfish, which I soon landed.

Captain Mitchell had run out to sea, so far we could hardly sight his boat. When he came in his flag was flying. He yelled something unintelligible to me about fish, and he looked excited; but not until we arrived at camp did I get the gist of what had happened. He had lost a hammer-head, also a Marlin, had another strike, and then caught a swordfish that went down deep and never rose until he was beaten. Two of the strikes the Captain got by trolling in front of sighted fish. This method to me is a sure and fascinating one. With our luck and the change of weather we were once more happy fishermen. Captain Mitchell's fish weighed two hundred and ninety-eight pounds and mine two hundred and thirty.

The weather is always a paramount consideration with a fisherman, especially him who fishes on the sea. We had one fairly good day, compared with the last week or so, but that was not by any means calm. Still we were able to troll out to sea half a dozen miles. We raised a Marlin with the teasers, and he promptly took my bait. He gave a splendid exhibition of lofty tumbling and skittering around on his tail, wearing out his strength so that I subdued him in half an hour. He was the largest fish so far for me.

Later I had another swordfish smash at the left teaser, but he did not come back. Following that we espied a hammer-head fin. Remembering how the two hammer-heads had outwitted me, I tried this one. He bit readily; nevertheless I could not hook him. Finally he took half

LEAPING STRIPED MARLIN (Plates xxviii to xli)
(Family Tetrapturus Albidus, commonly and erroneously called swordfish.
It is not a true swordfish, but a spearfish. The bill is round.)

PLATE XXVIII

PLATE XXIX

PLATE XXX

PLATE XXXI

Plate XXXII

PLATE XXXIII

PLATE XXXIV

Plate xxxv

PLATE XXXVI

PLATE XXXVII

Plate xxxviii

PLATE XXXIX

PLATE XL

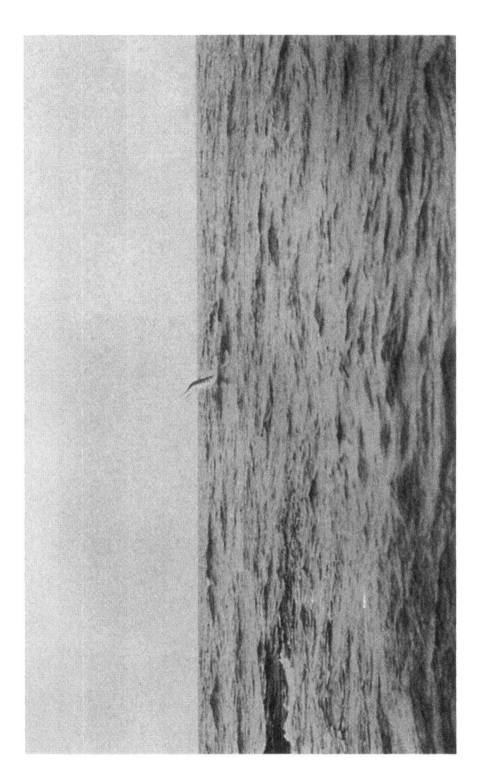

PLATE XLI

my bait and left. My conclusion was that this species of shark in New Zealand was very cunning.

Captain Mitchell lost a bait to a fish of some kind, and also fought a Marlin for a while, only to pull the hook. My Marlin, number nine for me, weighed an even three hundred pounds, giving me two pounds above Captain Mitchell's largest, a fact I made much of. "Well, Lucky Mitchell, I'm getting ahead of you," I averred complacently. "Better watch out, or I'll beat you as badly as you did me on the Rogue River in Oregon last fall. . . . Never will forgive your catching seventy-nine steelhead to my twenty-five!"

That evening in camp was warm and pleasant and still. Ominous clouds in the west loomed up, however, and in the night a heavy storm broke. How the wind howled in the *ti* trees and how the rain roared on my tent!

I remember with amusement an article sent me from some New Zealand newspaper. Two old gentlemen were discussing my visit and particularly the information that I was absorbing local color at Russell. One of them asked: "What you figure that air local color to mean, now?" His companion replied: "Aw, he's gettin' sunburnt. I know, because I've been at Russell."

Also I received a funny letter from a man who appeared somewhat annoyed at the tremendous importance apparently given me by the newspapers over my proposed swordfishing, and the amount of space given my tackle. In part he wrote: "See here, all this fuss about your coming seven thousand miles with high-priced new-fangled machinery to catch swordfish is sort of ridiculous. Sonny, I caught New Zealand swordfish before you were born, and did it with hairpins, too."

The old gentleman was as irate and sincere as he was ignorant. No doubt he meant the small silver fish, a few inches long, with a spear-like snout, my men called garfish and small boys misnamed swordfish; and he had no knowledge of the great broadsworded king of the seas.

An incident that I often recall as remarkable happened one day when we were running in from outside and had our flag flying. We stopped to maneuver round a fish. A big steamship, a freighter, was going to port; and seeing our flag and queer movements, the captain altered his course and bore down upon us until he ascertained we were not flying distress signals. I appreciated the good captain's loyalty to the code of the sea and regretted having unwittingly alarmed him.

After nine days of intermittent gales, storms, calms and downpours, we had a beautiful dawn that promised a beautiful day. Sunrise was rose and silver, shining on the hills where grazing sheep were silhouetted against the sky.

For a change we ran north through new channels, between islands different from those I had watched every day as we went to and fro, and each one seemed to add something to my growing delight in the wonderful Bay of Islands.

Outside to the north we found schools of yellowtail around a buoy. They were small and more suited to use as bait. We caught a dozen quickly. Some we essayed to keep alive in a large galvanized iron tank I had made for the purpose. We found that it worked splendidly, though it gave Arlidge and Pete Williams a lot of exercise with buckets. North from the buoy stood a large monumental rock called the Ninepin. It reminded me a little of El Capitan, the great sentinel rock in the Painted Desert of Arizona. An ocean swell rose green and gold over the base of the Ninepin and burst into roaring white chaos against the cliff. Contending strife of sea and rock! It was always present. There were schools of fish round the Ninepin, but no *kahawai*. From there we ran straight out to sea ten miles, which distance brought us some five or six miles off Cape Brett.

At first I thought we were going to have a smooth glassy sea, and had my eyes keen for broadbill fins. But a little breeze sprang up, ruffling the water. Still it was most wonderful compared with the last nine days, and I was accordingly grateful.

It turned out to be a great fishing day, the details of which were so many, exciting and confusing that I cannot recall them all. I trolled a yellowtail. This bait was not satisfactory, but it was better than a *kahawai*.

The color of the sea was deep dark blue, almost violet. Fleecy white clouds now and then shaded the warm sun. The breeze freshened. As I trolled along, suddenly I espied an albatross wheeling and sailing around our boat. I watched with absorbed and thrilling delight. During many years of fishing on the sea I had watched many birds, but never so grand a bird as this albatross. He had the sailing, shooting, rising and falling triangular flight of a shearwater, with every characteristic of that bird magnified. I was struck with the amazing fact that here I had the marvelous privilege of watching the albatross of the Antarctic. Truly I was far from home.

Early in the day I raised a Marlin, to be disappointed that the hook did not catch. Not long afterward, the teasers lured another from the purple depths. How he blazed in the clear water back of the boat, weaving to and fro before he hit the bait! The boatmen yelled. They surely were keen to catch fish. We got twenty-four jumps out of this swordfish. Not long after that I raised another and recorded eighteen for him. During the lunch hour, as the boatmen began to brew their tea, we let the boat drift. "Boys," I said, "I have a feeling you will miss your lunch."

Sure enough, before long I had a tremendous strike. I

hooked something that felt like the bottom of the sea. Yet it made fast runs, short and long. We thought I had a mako, and I worked accordingly. But my exceedingly hard exertion was rewarded only by a huge ugly reremai shark that gave us trouble at the boat. We signaled for the Captain's boat, and when it arrived we said we needed a few more men. My boatmen wanted to load this shark on board. I was not keen about that, but I did not object. Finally they got the brute on the stern and roped fast, as they imagined. Awhile later, when I hooked another Marlin, the shark began to thump and thresh. I was knocked out of my seat, nearly losing my rod. One of the guides was knocked off. Arlidge rescued my rod, sustaining a bruised foot. The monster then flopped over in the cockpit, almost filling it. Peter roped him down again, whereupon I went back to work on the swordfish, which, marvelous to relate, had not escaped. I was afraid the shark would break loose again and toss me overboard. Arlidge did get a bump as he was working the clutch. He shouted lustily and left his post in a hurry. Eventually the reremai quieted down and I landed my swordfish.

Then we made the discovery that Captain Mitchell was fighting a heavy fish. We ran over to learn that he had fastened to another reremai. I had a lot of fun telling the Captain to pull the brute up quickly. He was certainly engaged a long while, and punished his tackle considerably.

On the way in to Cape Brett the Captain had a Marlin take hold, waltz around the boat on his tail, and leap prodigiously to free himself at last. That ended a rather unusual day of bad luck for Captain Mitchell and good for me. We found we were more than an hour off the cape. I had raised six Marlin with the teasers. Once while fighting one of them my bait slipped up the line,

The Author Examining Crude Tackle Used by New Zealanders and Australians.
Note Reel Under Rod

PLATE XLII

Method of Playing Marlin Swordfish in Vogue in New Zealand Waters. The Fish Is Not Stopped and Fought, but Followed Out to Sea Until It Dies or Comes Up Exhausted

PLATE XLIII

and two Marlin charged it. "All off, boys," I called, slacking my line. "Those birds will cut me off."

We could see the purple and silver blazes, the bright stripes of the swordfish as they threshed around the bait. They left it, presently, and after all I saved my fish. This we regarded as the most exciting incident of an exciting day.

"Well," said Peter, his bronze face radiating enthusiasm, "the teasers are great. They raise the Marlins all right."

It seemed I had indeed established another fact—that the swordfish of the waters of the Antipodes could be raised to the surface by trolling. I was immensely pleased, for that must eventually change the whole fishing method around New Zealand. My fish weighed two hundred and eight, two hundred and twenty-four and two hundred and thirty-four pounds. The last one leaped twenty-one times.

We woke to a still better day, so far as weather and beautiful sea were concerned. It was, however, the thirteenth; and also I had reached my thirteenth Marlin! From a fisherman's standpoint, how was I ever going to overcome such monumental handicaps? I did not.

I had three beautiful strikes, and though two of them were extremely difficult strikes to handle, owing to the sudden long swift runs right from the start, I acted with all possible good judgment and skill. But not in any case did the hook hold. After all there *is* a great deal of luck about that. If a swordfish takes the bait between his jaws, not ravenously, and starts off with the head of the bait, containing the hook, toward the angler, it stands to reason that when the angler strikes he will either pull the bait out of the swordfish's mouth or the hook loose. Anyway, I did both things.

One of my Marlin was a big heavy fish, and he shot off

in a curve toward Captain Mitchell's boat, leaping wildly with the bait swinging six feet from his head. He had tangled in the leader. I saw it through his jaws. There was an enormous bag in the line, as the swordfish had run straight off, then suddenly doubled back. I simply could not hook him.

The last Marlin of the four I raised by teasers was a contrary fellow and very cunning and obviously not hungry. He shot to and fro behind the bait, a beautiful striped tiger of the sea. His pectorals stood out like jib booms on a ship. We ran away from him, teasing him to follow, which he did, even passing my bait; but he would not take it. Finally he sheered away, blazing like a silver-and-purple shield, and faded into the depths. After that I caught a reremai shark of about three hundred pounds weight, which we cut loose.

The day was not entirely lost, considering the pictures we obtained, and the raising of four more Marlin by the teasers.

At the cape, a half dozen or more boats caught nine Marlin. One boat had five fish on; and twice it had a double-header, which is two strikes simultaneously. In each case only one swordfish was landed. The drifting method evidently was prolific of strikes that day. Also there must have been plenty of swordfish, for I raised mine seven miles off the cape. What strong entrancement gripped me, trolling those deep unknown blue waters out there! Any moment I might raise an enormous black Marlin or a great sailfish or mako, or even a broadbill, not to think of some new species of fish.

The next day was the best day of all up to date, and naturally we expected much; especially to sight the sickle fins of a broadbill! But despite a smooth sea all day, not a sign! The sun shone hot. For the first time I fished without a coat or vest.

At three o'clock Pete sighted the long sharp tip of a Marlin tail. We ran over. He appeared asleep. Frank would have run closer, but I said, "If he is awake he'll see the teasers." When we got within two hundred feet, he woke up and swirled the water. Then he disappeared. In another moment, there he was behind the teasers, a great striped bird-like shape, quick as a flash. He was the largest I had seen up to then. Crossing behind the teasers two or three times, he sheered up, put his spear out of the water, and snapped in my bait. Away he shot! I let him go long enough, then struck, but the hook did not hold.

We saw the Captain have something of the same bad fortune. On the way in, near Piercy Rock, I sighted a mako. We caught him. Then a little later Pete sighted another, a larger one. We caught him. So the day ended well, after all. I had the fun of raising flag at the very end, and also of teasing Captain Mitchell and his boatmen.

My makos were small, as makos go, weighing one hundred and fifteen and two hundred pounds. I guessed the weight of the smaller at eighty-six pounds, and then made sure I had overestimated. These fish have the heaviest flesh of any I ever caught. They are tremendously well equipped to fight and destroy and live. While my men were gaffing the second mako, the first one, tied astern, bit the gaff rope through, and I almost lost this second and larger fish.

We left at daylight the following morning for Cavalli Islands, some twenty miles north up the coast. It was a delightful run in the clear rosy fresh morning. The sea was like glass. Everywhere schools of fish were darkening the water and sea birds were wheeling and fishing. We made the distance in a little over two hours.

The Cavallis are rough rugged islands dominated by a

large one reaching the dimensions of a mountain. The outer islands are all black rock, eaten to fantastic shapes by the hungry sea. There are two natural bridges, one almost equaling the superb arch at Piercy Island. This chain of islands reaches out miles into the open sea. Wash and boom of the surge are heard on all sides.

The point farthest out should have been a wonderful place for bait and fish, but we did not see any. Far off-shore, schools of *kahawai* showed black on the bright water. As we ran out, I sighted a Marlin weaving in, his tail just showing. We circled him; and what a rush he made at the teasers! They had to be pulled clear in to the boat, and then he bumped his bill into the stern. Finally I jerked my bait over him. How he whacked at it! Then securing it between his jaws, he flashed off.

This swordfish leaped seventeen times, and took forty minutes of hard fighting to subdue. He was game and strong.

We headed for the southeast, and trolled the miles away, now and then stopping awhile to drop down a live bait. But the sea seemed empty. Not until afternoon did I espy another Marlin fin. We got a bait in front of him, and he sailed after it. We were running fairly fast, and the swordfish, instead of weaving to and fro behind the bait, preparing to cross it, followed it precisely, trying to get it in his mouth. The bait was half out of water, which made the difficulty for the hungry Marlin. He afforded the boatmen much amusement, and I was thrilled and excited. For fifty yards or more he surged after my *kahawai* before he got it. Then he went down slowly and easily, turned to the left and kept pace with the boat. It was a wonderful strike. I waved for Captain Mitchell to come up on that side and be ready to photograph the swordfish. When I struck, he felt like a log, but he did not rise. We ran along for quite a distance. Then suddenly he plunged out, a very long, heavy, deep-striped Marlin, most wonderfully bright with silver and purple and green colors. His size amazed me and made the boatmen yell and rush for the cameras.

That swordfish leaped again and again, increasing his energy until it was tremendous. Soon he was throwing up so much water that I could not see him for splash and spray. Then he threw the hook, but even then kept on leaping. What a magnificent display! In all, he leaped clear eleven times; but he was on the surface during the whole short period after that first jump. I felt sort of stunned. This was the largest striped Marlin I ever saw, surely approaching five hundred pounds. There was no disregarding my bad luck. The loss affected me deeply, as my most cherished ambition for New Zealand waters was to catch one of those great Marlin.

CHAPTER VII

THE fourth perfect day made up most happily for
all the days of gale and rain. On the way in
from the sea, we became aware of a strange effect
in the sky. There was a haze through which the setting
sun shone dusky red. Through it the mountains were a
deep purple, and the water seemed on fire. As the sun
sank lower, these lights deepened and intensified until
the world of sky, earth and ocean was unreal, surpassingly beautiful, like a realm of dreams. Finally, the
sun turned magenta, and then the glow on the placid
waters was exquisitely lovely.

All this strange effect did not come from mere sunset,
but sunset through smoke of fires. Not until then did
I make the discovery that part of the golden grassy hills
of Orupukupuku had been burned over. They were
black, ghastly, smoking.

Upon arriving at camp, I found with some relief that
only half the island had been burned over. The wonderful slopes back of our grove of *ti* trees were still shining
and silvery.

We took our climb up the hills as usual, and Mrs. Mitchell observed that the larks were not singing. How strange I had not been quick to note that! But it appeared I was waiting until we attained the summit, there to see and hear everything.

Alas! not one lark sang for us. It was a melancholy omission. What had happened to the larks? These hideous black hilltops opposite answered that sinister question. The music of the sky birds, the joy of life that they vented so freely, had been quenched by the fire, the creeping line of red, the blowing pall of smoke. No doubt the larks knew those dread signs.

Next morning I was not awakened by the singing of larks. When I awoke I lay still awhile and listened. The laughing gulls made a great clamor, but there were no high sweet thrilling notes from the bird of the skies.

The hills had to be burned over by the sheep herders so that new grass would spring up the quicker. Sheep raising was a business. Who thought of the little larks in their nests? Only the frantic mother lark; and some such dreamer and nature lover as myself. If Orupuku-puku had belonged to me, there would not have been any burning of the waving grass on the silver hills.

As far as fishing was concerned, that day bid well to add more perfect weather to our mounting record. No wind! A warm hazed sun and a placid ocean! Captain Mitchell's boat was delayed longer than ours at catching bait. We were off Bird Rock while they were two miles behind, and lagging, I thought; but all at once I saw a big splash.

"Boys," I called, "the Captain has hooked something. Step on it and let's hustle back."

I saw more big white splashes, but not any distinct shape of a fish. When we got near the fish did not show.

Upon reaching the boat I yelled through the megaphone, "What're you fast to, Cap?"

The Captain appeared too busily engaged to reply, but one of the boatmen called, "Say, we've hooked the granddad of all the swordfish."

Whereupon I took my camera and climbed to the deck, motioning Frank to run closer. Presently I could see Captain Mitchell's line, and made a guess as to the whereabouts of the fish.

Suddenly the water bulged, opened with a sullen roar. A short black bill protruded, then an enormous glistening head, then the massive shoulders of a grand black Marlin. Slowly he seemed to propel himself upward into the air, but he was so heavy he could not clear the water. I snapped my camera while I let out the most stentorian yell I ever uttered over a fish.

Suddenly the swordfish sank. The splashing water subsided; then it opened again, and precisely as before the giant came out. I was ready with my camera, and also with a bellow that equaled my first. Then the extraordinary thing happened the third time, after which the swordfish went down.

In a blaze of thrilling excitement I directed the boatmen to run behind the Captain's boat and let me jump aboard. Soon I was beside him, and I believed it was well. Both boatmen were white with nervous excitement and Captain Mitchell looked as if he fully appreciated the situation. So I took charge of the operation of the boat and advised Captain Mitchell as best I could. I also yelled to my boatmen to run close and use my cameras.

Then began a magnificent fight with a truly grand fish. His heaves and leaps and runs, and the sound of the water as he came out and plunged back, the wild words of the boatmen, the yells of my men, the swift judgment

WORLD RECORD CATCH FOR ONE DAY

PLATE XLIV

AUTHOR'S WORLD RECORD STRIPED MARLIN, 450 POUNDS

PLATE XLV

I employed through the various situations, and lastly the appalling beauty and wonder of that fish—all were registered in my mind, but never to be recalled clearly.

Yet I remember vividly my sensations as the Captain drew the wire leader to my hands, and I could not risk holding it. Time after time this happened. I held a little harder every time, until at last came that most frightfully strained moment for me when I heaved the swordfish closer, closer, closer, and at the same time told each man what to do. Up the grand fish came. Black! Huge! Not a stripe on him! He had a short blunt bill, low black dorsal, body as large as that of an ox, tail wider than a door. His eye gleamed, he rolled heavily; the leader and hook held. I heaved with all my might. "Gaff him!" I yelled, "over the back! Quick!"

When the gaff went in I leaped down and helped hold that wagging handle. The swordfish sent up mountains of water. Both Hodgson and I were lifted, thrown, dragged, but we held him while the other boatman lassoed the monstrous looming tail.

Then I fell back, exhausted and spent, to congratulate the Captain. He was wet with sweat, dishevelled and almost at the point of collapse. The battle had not been so long as others I had engaged in, but it had been strenuous, and, through emotion, fearfully wearing on the nerves.

It took both crews to pull that swordfish upon the stern of the Captain's boat. Then we ran out to sea, as if such a capture was all in the day's work. Three miles out Captain Mitchell raised and hooked a striped Marlin that led him a chase. I was about to follow when I espied a sharp dark sickle tail above the water.

"We've got trouble of our own, boys," I said, pointing. "Run over to that one."

When within two hundred feet, the tail disappeared.

In another instant the purple wings and bird-like shape of a swordfish appeared, as if by magic, behind our teasers.

We went through the usual exciting procedure, and things turned out well. It was only when this swordfish began to leap that a great difference manifested itself. He leaped out like a greyhound. He went high into the air, fully fifteen feet over the water, and all of thirty feet in a long curve. We had to chase him full speed. Each leap appeared more wonderful, higher, longer, until they were incredible.

He leaped seventeen times in succession, the last of which was marvelous in the extreme. I never had seen such an exhibition. So many leaps, such increasing speed, height, distance; such blazing of purple, silver, bronze; such quivering of body, wagging of bill, and sweeping of tail were surely the magnification of all other performances.

After that he slowed down, sank deep and gave me an hour of very hard labor. Then he made another display of leaping, showing seven more times.

When I finally had the Marlin on board our boat, I beheld the Captain approaching. His men signaled, and we were soon within hailing distance, but that did not suit the Captain. He had the boats come to a stop together. His face was beaming.

"Most extraordinary thing!" he exclaimed. "By gad! I never saw the like. Our teasers raised two Marlin, one the usual size and striped, the other a big black fellow. They charged the teasers together. Then the big black one flashed at the other, and rammed him terribly. I saw the bill go in. The struck Marlin leaped out terrifically, and the black devil followed him. For half a mile that struck swordfish leaped out every few seconds; . . . most extraordinary thing I ever saw."

"Well!" I ejaculated. "What do you think of that?
. . . I just had something wonderful happen, too. Let's
go back to camp before one of these fish sinks us."

Mitchell's black Marlin was as grand on nearer view
as he had been while leaping; but the wildness and
blaze had faded with his life. He was a fish of the most
graceful lines that ever blessed my sight. Verily he was
a black-opal-and-silver hue with leaden fins. Nowhere
the slightest mark of a stripe! The large round pupil of
his eye matched the color of his fins and the cornea re-
tained all the iridescence of his body. His fins were perfectly turned to the shape of delicate pointed scythes,
with which he had slashed through the seas. How wonderfully nature had combined his ponderous size and
majesty with beauty and grace! His shoulders were
magnificent, his depth incredible, his bulk carrying clear
to his enormously wide tail.

There was a most remarkable contrast between this
fish and the striped Marlin. First in the absence of
purple stripes; secondly, in the short heavy blunt bill, it
not being much longer than a foot; thirdly, in the low
short dorsal fin; and fourthly, in the lower maxillary,
which was also very short and which curved down, like
a beak. This last feature is peculiarly that of a black
Marlin. His pectoral fins were narrow, curved and very
long. The queer little appendages between them, that
in a sailfish are very extended in length and delicate as
rapiers, were scarcely six inches long. They resembled
feelers. What use could such a tremendous fish find in
those two feather-like projections? I had no idea.

He measured five and a half feet in girth and twelve
and a half feet in length; a remarkable length considering the shortness of his bill. His tail spread forty-seven
inches, and he weighed six hundred and eighty-five
pounds.

To that date, this was the world record for both flat and round bill swordfish. The time of capture was something over two hours, a very short fight for such a marvelous fish. No doubt the effort required to propel his huge bulk into the air told greatly upon his strength. We differed as to number of leaps he made, but I remembered twenty-three. Never shall I forget one of them! It was breath-taking to see him, and nerve wrecking for me pulling on the leader and risking a break!

Fighting a great game fish is hard work, but it is not the hardest connected with the sport. With the strike and the following battle there is an excitement that makes time fly and labor seem nothing. Only when severe exhaustion and pain become manifest does the mind dwell upon the physical side of it.

I have encountered but few anglers who could stand this game for any great length of time. The way we fish for sailfish, swordfish and tuna involves a searching of the sea, running miles and miles to locate a particular fish or find where a school is surfacing. The glare of the bright water is perhaps the hardest thing to endure, unless it is the vain hunt, day after day, without sighting what you want.

Of course, in New Zealand waters we did not have this vain hunt, for we were always raising swordfish or getting strikes. We met, however, the other discomforts and endurance-testing features. Foremost of these was the rough sea. We had ten days of rocking boats, that each day, along in the afternoon, made things almost unendurable. Then followed nine perfect days which spoiled us. After that we struck a windy day. It appeared only a breeze when we started out, and deceived us. When we were miles offshore a strong wind blew down on us, kicking up a tremendous sea. At first the sensation of trolling over great blue white-crested roar-

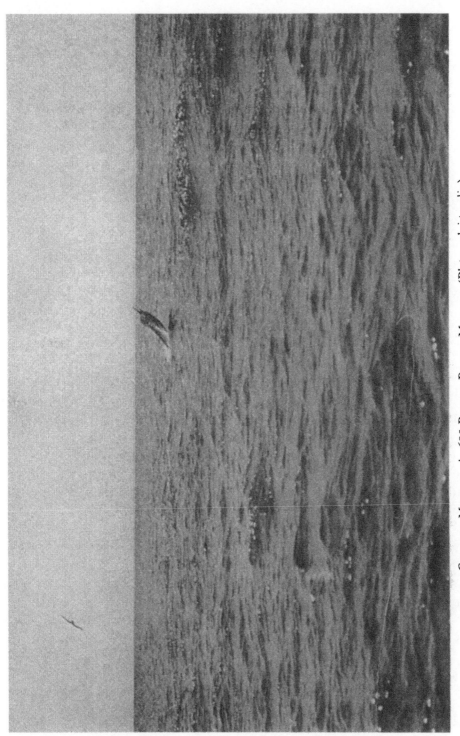

CAPTAIN MITCHELL'S 685-POUND BLACK MARLIN (Plates xlvi to xlix)

(*This is a distinct species from the striped variety and is still unclassified. The name Black Marlin was bestowed by the author.*)

PLATE XLVI

PLATE XLVII

PLATE XLVIII

PLATE XLIX

ing billows was most thrilling. There was the keen zest
to see a swordfish come shooting through the swells at our
teasers; and then the wonder of having him leap across
the blue hollows and out of the curling combers.

Captain Mitchell did hook one that danced over the
sea in a most amazing way. It was so rough, however,
that I could not hold my camera level. In fact I could
not do anything save hold on to the boat.

That night I was worn out, and as sore in body as if I
had been beaten with a club. When I awoke I could not
sit up. My back seemed broken. I had to work around
sideways and finally got to a sitting posture, so I could
dress. After some brisk exercise in the cool dawn I got
rid of the soreness.

My Marlin swordfish, numbers fifteen, sixteen, seventeen, caught during the last few days prior to the windy
one, weighed two hundred and fifty-eight, two hundred
and seventy-eight, and two hundred and fifty pounds,
respectively. I also captured a five-hundred-pound
reremai, an achievement I did not care to repeat. He
was a strong heavy brute and hard to lift.

On February nineteenth we scoured the smooth opal
sea all morning, and ran all over the territory we knew,
looking for fins. But not a fin! We did not raise a
Marlin, either. At the lunch hour we stopped the engine
and drifted. The English boatmen all loved their tea
and it took half an hour to brew it, and another half hour
to eat their lunch. My sandwich and apple required
only about five minutes to dispose of. After that I put
out a live bait, a big *kahawai*, and let out over a hundred
feet of line, in the hope that while drifting I might get
a mako strike.

It was warm and pleasant on the sea, and the gentle
rocking of the boat was not conducive to a wide-awake
habit. To try to keep from dozing I watched the gannets

and shearwaters. Suddenly I saw a big white splash about a mile off. I watched. Then a huge mako shot up white in the sunlight, turned clear over and dived back into his element.

"Boys," I called, "I saw a mako jump. Hook up and run over there."

We did so, and stopped as near the place as I could calculate, where I put my bait down again. Nothing happened. I was slipping into a doze when I thought my line jerked through my fingers; still I could not be sure. After I had relaxed vigilance again the same thing happened.

"I'll be dog-goned!" I soliloquized, somewhat puzzled. "Did something happen or was I dreaming as usual?"

Some moments of tense waiting were unproductive. I had only imagined my line had jerked. So I settled back again in my comfortable chair, just about as content as a man could well be.

Then came a tremendous jerk on my line. It whipped out of my hand. My reel spun round, though I had the light drag on. Frantically I bent over to grasp the rod and free the drag. Then the line paid out swiftly in a wonderful strike.

"Gee, boys!" I shouted. "There's something doing here."

"Mako!" exclaimed Frank brightly.

"Sure that's a mako!" added Peter.

"Well, maybe so; but there's a familiar feel about the way this fellow does business," I replied grimly, watching my line slip off. "Signal to the Captain's boat."

By the time the Captain had run up close behind us I was hooked to a heavy fast fish, and I had begun to suspect something too good to be true. Two hundred yards of line in one run! If that was mako work, I had to confess he was better than I thought him.

"Mako, and a big one!" yelled Frank, as we ran after the fish.

"Sure, that's the way a mako acts," said Peter, with great satisfaction.

"Ahuh! Well, you boys grab the cameras and look out," I replied. "This bird I've hooked is going to fly."

We were running full speed. My line was still slipping off the reel, and a long stretch of it had come to the surface. More of it showed.

"Look out! He's coming up!" I shouted. "Get ready! . . . Oh, it's a *broadbill!*"

I was not so astonished. I had been wondering. But I was tremendously elated, and tingled all over. The boatmen whooped, and from the Captain's boat behind rose wild yells of excitement.

"Watch sharp. He's coming out again," I called.

The second leap was enough to dazzle any boatmen, let alone two who had never seen a broadbill. It was a forward jump, quite high and long, allowing us time to see his bronze bulk, his wide black tail, his huge shiny head and waving sword. I thought my boatmen had gone crazy; and the manifestations of the occupants of the other boat were no better.

The broadbill did not show again. After several long amazing runs, that made us hustle to keep pace with him, he sounded, and the hard fight was on. He kept steadily out to sea, and gained line despite all my efforts and the help of the boat. After a while he sounded deep, fully a thousand feet, and there he anchored himself. I had the heart-breaking task of pumping him up inch by inch.

"Broadbills are alike, in any old sea!" I exclaimed, during this procedure. It took me half an hour to work him to the surface.

To make a long story short, I fought him with all the strength I had, and with all the play the great tackle would stand. Toward the end of the fight he sounded even deeper, and this time he quit down there. I knew it, but did not tell the boatmen. I labored strenuously, with keen calculation and some conservation of strength, to lift him from the depths. How familiar the heaving chest, the wet face, arms, neck, breast, the aching back and blistered hands! Could it really be true that I had caught a broadbill, way out in New Zealand? At last I had him up so that we could see the gleaming pale color, then the massive shape, the long fierce-looking sword. What the boatmen said I could never remember, but it was a medley of whirling words. I had the sword-fish whipped, and he gave little trouble at the boat.

Captain Mitchell and his crew came close to look and to yell, to congratulate me and give a few whoops for New Zealand waters.

We were about four miles off the cape. Loading the swordfish, we ran in to exhibit him to the seven or eight boats fishing there. I shall not soon forget the expression of those anglers. Such a marvelous and amazing fish as the broadbill had never been imagined by them. We then went on to the camp, which we reached before sun-down and in time for some picture-taking. We all made guesses as to the weight of my fish; and I, for once, hit it correctly, four hundred pounds even!

The boat crews were keen to take the fish to Russell to exhibit. I not only consented to that, but told them to have the broadbill cut up so everybody in the village could eat some of it. They returned with the glowing ac-counts of the week-end visit at home. The broadbill swordfish created a sensation in the little town; and as late as eleven o'clock at night people were inspecting the fish with torches.

A couple of days later—both of which were unproductive of everything but good luck for me—we came in to the cape about four o'clock. There were fifteen boats around the great rock, most of them near, some far off; and five of them were fast to fish, working out to sea with the anglers sitting comfortably in chairs on the bows. Not a bent rod among the five! Eight of the other boats had one or two swordfish on board.

This circumstance might not have been remarkable for Cape Brett anglers, but it was exceedingly so for me. Manifestly the Marlin had come in to feed that day. They were all small fish for those waters, and of a uniform size, around two hundred pounds. I had not the slightest doubt that large fish had been hooked and lost.

We trolled twice round the island without raising anything, then proceeded to Bird Rock. The sun was now low and red in the west. The sea, colored like an opal, was without a ripple. Acres of *kahawai* were darkening the surface, and myriad little white gulls were hovering and fluttering over them. The fish raised a white caldron on the water and a sound exactly like a brook rushing over stones. The birds were screaming. Every now and then the *kahawai* leaped as one fish to escape some enemy underneath, and made a prolonged roar in the water.

I trolled round, while Captain Mitchell let down a dead yellowtail for bait, and drifted. Soon he had a strike and hooked something heavy that moved away slowly, without showing. Another boat came along and followed the Captain's out to sea.

Meanwhile I tried letting down a live bait, which presently was seized by what turned out to be a forty-pound yellowtail. I tried again without reward. The sun was setting, the time nearly six o'clock, and Captain Mitchell was working farther out to sea. I began to suspect he had attached himself to another black Marlin or a huge reremai.

Suddenly I espied a thin long sickle fin quite near the rock. Not long did it take us to throw out teasers and draw a *kahawai* in front of the waving tail. It vanished. Next instant a purple-finned Marlin rushed our teasers, then my bait. He took it, spat it out. Then he flashed back, from one teaser to the other, then at my bait again. But he refused to touch the *kahawai*. I reeled in to put on a yellowtail. Meanwhile we were running quite fast, with the teasers out, and the Marlin knocking at them with his bill. It was great fun and most exciting. As we passed near a school of *kahawai* the swordfish left the teasers and sheered at the *kahawai*. They smashed the water. Then he came back at us and chased the teasers clear to the rudder. I dragged my yellowtail over his back time and again. Finally he left us. But presently he rose again farther out, making a ripple and showing a foot of his slender blue tail. We headed him as before, and precisely as before he charged us, this time going straight for my bait. He took it, went down, and came back for the teasers. I struck him and had a hard tussle with him, deep down. Captain Mitchell returned just as we were trying to lasso the tail of my Marlin, and had the fun of seeing us thoroughly drenched by the spouts of water.

"Lost my fish!" called Mitchell, tragically. "Big black Marlin. Hook pulled out. By gad! he was a lunker! . . . Terrible day of bad luck for me! Broke one rod, bent my reel ——"

"But you hooked the fish," I interrupted. "I was watching, you lucky fisherman. Can't understand why your black Marlin did not jump aboard your boat."

We reached our little bay in the ruddy afterglow of

sunset, and went ashore with our fish. They proved to be splendid specimens of the striped Marlin, mine weighing two hundred and ninety-two and the Captain's three hundred and two. He was disconsolate because I had not hooked the big black Marlin he lost. That was nothing to what I was.

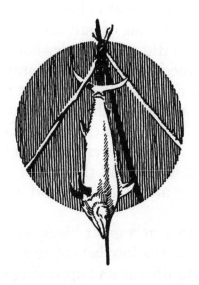

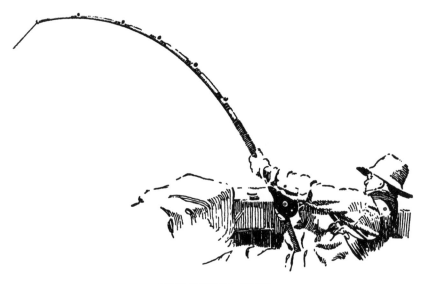

CHAPTER VIII

THE Cavalli Islands strongly impressed me as being a remarkably favorable place for big game fish. I clung to that belief. We had not seen any *kahawai* or other schools of bait there, but as we had left early in the day I did not consider our failure as conclusive. So I planned to go again and stay overnight.

We went. I never shall forget that trip. We arrived there about the middle of the afternoon. What a difference from our former visit! The sea was alive with schools of bait. Big fish were smashing the water, gulls were screaming, all around there were continuous sound and the haunting moan and roar and wash of the restless sea.

I had my chance at a great black Marlin. He loomed a massive purple shadow behind my bait, became clear and sharp, a magnificent and appalling sight. He struck viciously at my bait—took it—sheered away—while I shook in my seat. But he felt the hook and threw it. . . . That loss colored my thoughts for long. But the late afternoon and sunset were reward, almost for any loss, let alone that of an incurable fisherman.

All day the smoke from forest fires had blown out over the sea, and that, with the gathering clouds, had prepared a beautiful veil through which the red sun burned. There were lights on the water that did not belong on land or sea. The shafts of rock stood up bronze and gold through the smoke. The schools of *kahawai* spread and rippled on the dark water, every now and then crashing a wide white area of spray that turned into a million diamonds of gold and fire.

Far out a storm gathered, a dark violet cloud massed low above the horizon; and in the west the sun became lost in a haze of dusky rose. I seemed to smother in the fragrance of burning autumn leaves. My ears were filled with the low sad surge of the sea. Sunset, twilight, dusk; then we ran round the main island to a protected bay.

After supper we went ashore in the dingy. A strong breeze had blown away the smoke and clouds, and from a clear sky the white moon shone. Again, for the thousandth time, I walked alone on a lonely beach, listening to the grating roar of the pebbles that the sullen surge drew down. Lines of Matthew Arnold's great poem, "Dover Beach," lingered in my mind.

Next day there were all kinds of beautiful weather—calm, still, hot, windy and squally, bright sunlight on a blue white-crested sea and dark purple shadows sailing like ships on the swells. All day I had in my charmed ears the song of the surge. That is to say, I heard this low music of the sea during those rather infrequent periods when I was not fighting a fish. Yet sometimes even then I was aware of the heave of the billows against the hollow cliffs and over the ragged reefs.

About two-thirty o'clock, when I regretfully remembered we were a long three hours' run from camp, I had two swordfish and one mako aboard the boat. Captain Mitchell's boat appeared rounding the lower rock, where we had found bait so plentiful, and I thought I had better remind him that we must soon leave. Then I was rather glad to observe that he had just hooked a fish and was pumping away in his usual energetic manner. "Good!" I soliloquized: "I can't start back without the Cap! . . . Wonder what the lucky lobster has got fast to now. . . . Looks slow and heavy to me."

I watched to see if the fish broke water, but it did not. Gradually the Captain's boat worked out. "Humph!" I said. "I'll have to follow him if that keeps up."

During the next hour I was pretty strenuously engaged myself, mostly on a fine Marlin that I caught, and for a short while on something heavy that I lost. Both my boatmen were keen on records, and wanted me, and incidentally their boat, the *Alma G.*, to beat the best day's record for Cape Brett boats, and for that matter any of the fishing-resort boats. I had then already succeeded; yet it was not a difficult matter to induce me to keep fishing; not at that wonderful place!

When, however, the Captain's boat got several miles out I decided we must follow him. This we did, and in short order slowed down within shouting distance.

"Hey, Cap," I yelled, "don't you know we must start back?"

"Can't help it," he returned; "I've hung on to a wolloper."

"So I see. Well, hand it to him. I'll go back and keep an eye on you. If you don't come in soon, we'll hunt you up."

Returning to the vicinity of the rocks, where the surge boomed and the gulls screamed and the *kahawai* lashed the water white, I was soon engaged upon another swordfish. He did not appear obliging, for he took us in the opposite direction from the Captain's boat; and he fought me to a standstill for one hour.

The time was four o'clock. We could just catch sight of the Captain's boat; and when I had fished awhile longer all we could see was the mast. Both boatmen averred the boat was returning. I did not think so, but I waited until the mast disappeared.

"Mitchell is tangled up with another big fish," I said to the men. "Hook her up and let's find him."

We ran northeast four miles before I sighted the other boat, just a speck on the horizon. It was fully ten miles from the rock where Captain Mitchell had hooked the fish. This, of course, argued in favor of something unusual.

We sped on, and soon I sighted a big blue fin cutting the swells. It belonged to a swordfish of uncertain species and size. We threw out teasers and bait, and tore at full speed in his direction. The sharp tail showed only at the tops of swells. From that way of riding the waves I knew him to be a Marlin. Soon I espied his long dark shape. We were fully three hundred feet distant; yet as Frank slowed down the engine that swordfish saw our shining teasers, and he vanished.

"Boys, he's coming!" I yelled. "Look sharp!"

The position of the boat was such that astern the water was dazzling bright with sunlight, making it impossible to catch a glimpse of either teasers or bait. But suddenly the line by which I was dragging the bait was ripped out of my hands.

"Wow! He's got it."

So incredibly swift was this swordfish that I had just time to grasp my rod when the line whipped taut. Like lightning in his swiftness the fish shot forward. I shut down on the drag, at the same moment telling Frank full speed ahead. Seldom, if ever, did I see or hear a reel whiz so fast. Almost like a rifle bullet the swordfish sped, never showing once on the surface. At four hundred and fifty yards, which he took in a few seconds while we were running at top speed after him, the hook pulled out.

Slowly I wound in my line. Both boatmen were downcast. They had never known a fish to take line like that. "Some swordfish!" I said, ponderingly. "And I'm inclined to think it was a black Marlin."

Half an hour later we ran up to the other boat, that for most of this time I had watched with great interest. But not until we arrived close did I find out anything.

First I saw an enormous fish tail sticking up out of the water, and roped to the boat. The breadth of those black flukes, the huge thickness of the tail, sort of stunned me. I could not look. It appeared there were four very much exhausted and excited men on that boat, particularly Captain Mitchell. He was haggard, wet, dishevelled.

"Just gaffed him," he called thickly. "Had an awful fight. When he came up so I could see how big he was, it scared me out of my wits. . . . Good Heavens! take a look at that swordfish!"

I was looking with all my might, though all I could make out was the huge tail and the long shadowy shape hanging down. For a few moments, everyone except me talked at once, and nobody knew what was said.

Presently the four men, using a block and tackle, began to haul the black Marlin aboard the wide stern. As slowly the glistening opal monster was hoisted out of the water I was further amazed, staggered; and finally, when they got his shoulders and head clear, I was overwhelmed.

This Marlin was as large round as a hogshead, and so

enormously long that tail and head projected far over each side of the eleven-foot beam stern.

Hoarsely shouting some rattled encomium of wonder and admiration, I subsided into my chair, suddenly weak. In my fishing day I had seen some great fish carried aboard or towed back to camp; but this one made comparison cheap. For twelve years, ever since I first knew about Marlin, I had dreamed of such a fish. Of course I was glad Captain Mitchell had caught it, just as I knew he was glad when I beat his tuna record with my seven-hundred-and-fifty-eight pounder; nevertheless, the sight and realization of this black Marlin was a jolt. I knew it would weigh one thousand pounds.

We were twenty-five miles from camp. The sun was setting, the sea and wind were rising, and the moon showed pale in the eastern sky. Dusk mantled the waste of waters, the afterglow faded, the moon soared, making a brilliant track over the billows, and the dew fell heavily, almost as thick as rain. By eight o'clock we picked up the Ninepin Rock, then Redhead, and lastly the lighthouse flash on Cape Brett. By nine we were in camp, wet, tired out, hungry as bears, and quite insane over the day. The stories of Captain Mitchell's boatmen, Bill and Warne, were interesting as phenomena of wild precipitant speech, but scarcely rational at that moment. The Captain, usually so cool and practical, like most Englishmen, was more wrought up than I had ever known him.

"We saw some bait close to that rock," he said. "We ran over close, and I threw my yellowtail over. It was dead, but I thought I'd try it anyway. By gad! something took it right off, slow and easy. I let that fish run off two hundred yards of line. When I struck he felt as solid as Gibraltar. I couldn't do anything with him. We followed him, but I fought for all I was worth.

When you came out the first time I hadn't seen the fish, didn't know it was a swordfish, and had no idea it was so big. After you left it jumped half out. He looked mighty thick, even far away; but I didn't see him well. Later he jumped twice, and I thought the boatmen were crazy. Next thing another black Marlin came up, fully as large as the one on my hook. He shot by the boat and back again under my line. I was sure he'd cut it. No doubt this was the mate to the one I'd hooked. He seemed wild and mad. Oh! if you had only stayed with us! You might have caught him.

"Well, I worked harder than ever before, on any fish, even my big tuna, yet I couldn't stop the beggar. He was game, fast, incredibly strong. He would take short quick runs, down deep and high up. Once he had off almost all my line; all except thirty yards! I had been fighting him nearly four hours when he took a last short run and stopped! After that I found I could hold him, lead him, drag him. Soon I brought him up. He looked so tremendous that I was scared weak. I had not dreamed of such a fish. I nearly fell out of my chair. Bill hauled on the leader, and Warne gaffed him. Then Bill reached over with a rope and got it round the fish's tail, but not in a loop or knot. Bill fell down in the cockpit, yelling for help. Crack! went the gaff. Bang! Bang! Bang! The huge swordfish tail jarred the whole boat and half filled it with water. We were deluged. Warne got another rope and got that on the banging tail, same as Bill's. He was lifted off his feet and slammed to the floor of the cockpit. I left my rod and jumped to their aid. Then the three of us lay flat on our backs, feet braced on the gunwale, and strained every nerve and muscle to hold that fish. Morton had wit enough to grab another rope; making a noose, he threw it tight around the tail and then to one of the posts. Only when we had his tail in a noose did I recover. . . . By gad! it was an awful fight!"

Not until next morning did I have a good look at this great Marlin, and though I had prepared myself for something extraordinary, I had not done it justice.

It was considerably larger than Captain Mitchell's six-hundred-and-eighty-five-pound swordfish, but of different shape and color; and not anything like the other for symmetry and beauty. In fact this one hardly seemed beautiful at all. It was almost round, very fat and full clear down to the tail, and solid as a rock. Faint dark stripes showed through the black opal hue. The bill was short, and as thick as a spade handle at the point. The hook of the lower maxillary had been blunted or cut off in battle. Huge scars indented the broad sides—many of them. The length was twelve feet, eight inches; the girth six feet, two inches; the spread of tail, four feet; and the weight nine hundred and seventy-six pounds. It had to be taken to Russell and cut into three pieces in order to weigh it at all. What an unbelievable monster of the deep! What a fish! I, who had loved fish from earliest boyhood, hung round that Marlin absorbed, obsessed, entranced and sick with the deferred possibility of catching one like it for myself. How silly such hope! Could I ever expect such marvelous good luck? Yet I knew as I gazed down upon it that I would keep on trying as long as strength enough was left me. That ought to be a good many years, I figured. Oh, the madness of a fisherman! The strange something that is born, not made!

The stomach of the leviathan contained two *kahawai* and nine redsnapper, all of large size. This old swordfish must have had to cruise round most of the day and part of the night to satisfy his enormous appetite. But how did he ever catch those swift little fish? He had to be faster than they. Considering his bulk and the displacement of water necessary when he moved, such swiftness seemed inconceivable. Perhaps he united cunning with speed, and maneuvered under a school of fish, suddenly to shoot upward and whack right and left with his bill. That was only a conjecture. We found many snapper in the stomachs of Marlin, and most of them had been speared. Nature knows how to endow her fish, as well as all other creatures, with the instincts and powers necessary to their self-preservation and reproduction.

Naturally the capturing of the first true swordfish in New Zealand waters, and the two enormous black Marlin, created a sensation all over the island. Some of my former remarks in Wellington, Auckland and Russell, that had been received rather skeptically, were recalled with sincerity; and New Zealand anglers began to wake up.

Peter Gardiner, one of the pioneers of sea angling in New Zealand, called on me at my camp, bringing his homemade tackle for my inspection. The reel was a ponderous affair, with levers and brakes that might have served for automobile clutches. The rod was of native wood, long, thick, clumsy; and the guides were huge rings, wrapped underneath. The line was a 36 Cuttyhunk, wholly unsuitable to the rest of the tackle. Mr. Gardiner, who had written me to California about New Zealand fishing, proved to be a frank, intelligent and practical angler, anxious to learn all he could. I explained the faults of his tackle, and then showed him my own and how it worked. He was amazed and keen; but he could not quite see why the triple gang hook was not better than the single hook. Only time and personal experience can prove this fact to anglers who have started

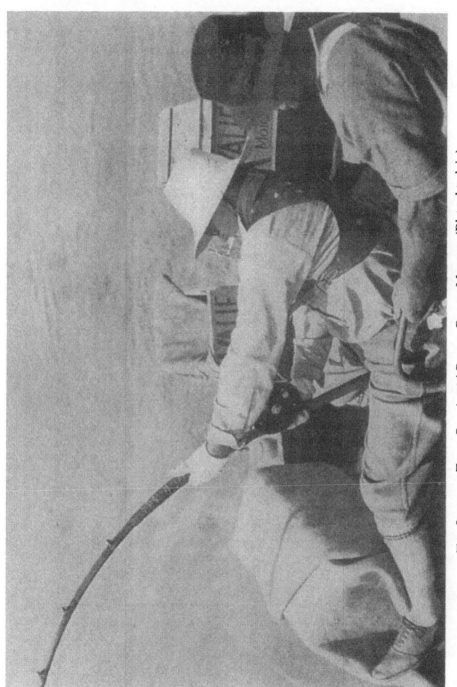

THE STORY OF ZANE GREY'S 704-POUND BLACK MARLIN (Plates l to lxix)

PLATE L

PLATE LI

PLATE LII

Plate LIII

Plate LIV

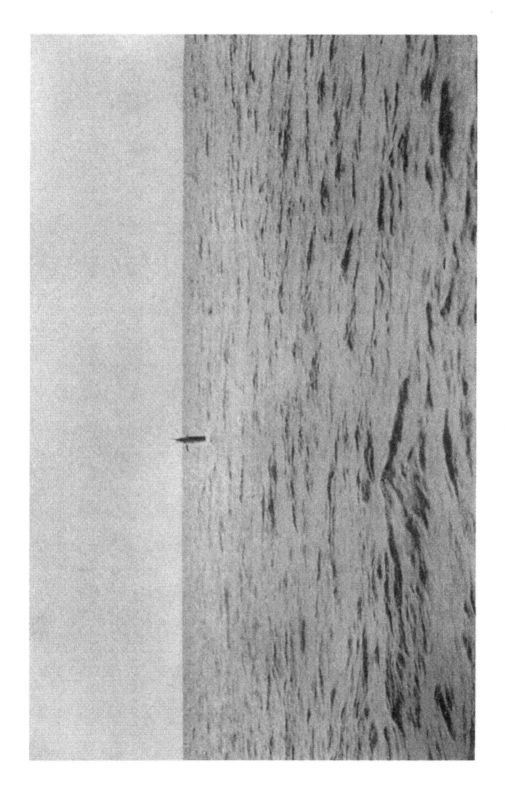

PLATE LV

PLATE LVI

PLATE LVII

PLATE LVIII

PLATE LIX

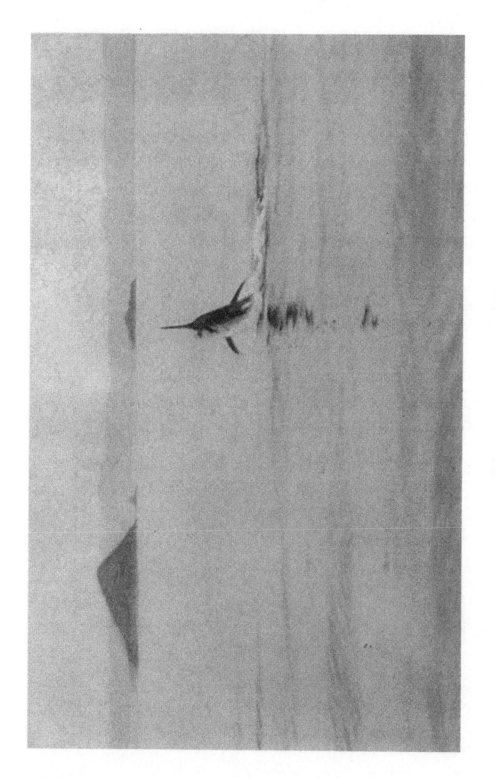

PLATE LX

PLATE LXI

PLATE LXII

PLATE LXIII

PLATE LXIV

PLATE LXV

PLATE LXVI

PLATE LXVII

PLATE LXVIII

Plate LXIX

wrong. The English are slow to change. Yet Captain Mitchell and Alma Baker, both conservative British sportsmen, had been quick to see the advantage of American method and tackle, and to adopt them.

Following Mr. Gardiner's visit there were two more anglers called on us from their camp at Deep Water Cove. They were from Sydney, and had been fishing off Cape Brett for a couple of weeks.

One of them, Mr. Lamb, had a tale of woe to unfold. The day before he had hooked an exceedingly large fish, which upon breaking water proved to be a black Marlin of giant dimensions; but he could not do anything with it. His boat followed it out to sea for miles, while he labored all he could with his tackle. At last the fish slowed up and quit fighting; but it could not be lifted. The tackle was not equal to it. So the boatman cut the line!

"But, Mr. Lamb, did you expect to catch such a heavy fish with your kind of tackle?" I inquired. "If so, you attempted the impossible."

"I'm convinced of that, and have come over to find out where we can get such tackle as you and Captain Mitchell and Mr. Baker use," he replied.

Whereupon we had the pleasure of showing the great Coxe reels, the Murphy hickory rods, and the Hardy Bros. English tackle.

We had other news that day, quite pleasing in a way, though it concerned an angler's bad luck. Some men were returning from a trip out to Hen and Chickens Islands, south of Cape Brett, when one of them had a terrific strike. The fish came up, showing the long sharp blade of a broadbill swordfish, and with one long rush it took all the angler's line. How familiar that sounded to my ears!

We had been so misled and enchanted by the perfect weather that we forgot there could be any other kind. To our dismay one sunset darkened sinisterly into storm. Next day the hard gale returned, reminding us of that past ten-day period we had found so irksome. We had wind and more wind. On the second night the gale abated, the clouds vanished over the hills, the full moon soared white and beautiful over bay and islands.

We planned to take a three-day trip to the Cavallis, and were most eager and enthusiastic. Several times during the night I awoke, to be thrilled by the almost absolute stillness. With the tide far at ebb, there was not a ripple on the beach.

The gulls did not, as usual, stir me at dawn. It was a roar of rain on the tent; I was flabbergasted, and thought I was dreaming. I arose to a dark-gray sky and beating rain. The wind came hard from the southeast, directly from the sea; and the boatmen said, "Dirty weather!"

Toward noon it cleared somewhat. The clouds broke, the sun shone, the wind lulled, and our hopes revived. How strange that Captain Mitchell and I could not be happy except in the act of fishing! Alma Baker rather welcomed a windy day, so that he could attend to his correspondence.

After lunch Captain Mitchell and I started out. Once round the corner of the island bay we ran into a good stiff breeze. A big white-crested swell was running. The rents in the gray scud, showing the blue sky, closed ominously. Out at Bird Rock the sea swelled tumultuously. We saw four fishing boats from Deep Water Cove, all drifting. Each boat had a Marlin swordfish lashed to the stern. About the same time Frank espied a big blue fin cutting the waves. That surely belonged to a large Marlin. He disappeared, however, before we could get a bait in front of him.

We found trolling about in that heavy sea about as uncomfortable a procedure as imaginable for fishing. Still we persisted for an hour, while the other boats drifted, and the scud thickened, the gray mists gathered over Cape Brett, and dull rainbows flashed in the spray toward the sun track on the water. Finally we tried drifting with a live bait. Promptly I got fast to a small but hard-fighting mako. While we were loading it on the boat, Captain Mitchell passed and yelled that he had just had a strike.

"Had a bunch of piper on for bait," he shouted, hands to his mouth. "Good hard strike!"

Piper are small slim fish that frequent the shoal waters of the bay. They are very good to eat. The Captain, however, had to try them out as bait.

It struck me again, even more significantly and forcibly, what a wonderful place for big game fish! The weather scarcely mattered. Probably if we had been out during the middle of the day we would have caught several swordfish. The rain set in again, and soon the Deep Water Cove boats left for camp.

I sat in my chair, with heavy coat on, and wrapped in burlap sacks, holding to my line, waiting for a bite. It seemed a rather ludicrous situation. The boat rose on the big swells; it pitched, it rocked, it smacked; it rode the great rollers that came every now and then. Spray whipped up from under the stern and wet my face. The harder gusts of wind brought stinging cold rain. It pelted me. The water ran off my hat and shoulders in sheets. Sometimes I could scarcely see. We drifted a mile beyond Bird Rock, then ran back to try again.

All the bad conditions increased. I grew wet and chilled. One hand was numb; but just as I was about to haul in and quit, something slow and heavy took my bait. A flash of fire, a tingle, a galvanic shock swept over me. Instantly the discomfort vanished, as if by magic. Marvelous fact, I had a strike! But the fish let go, and gradually I relaxed. I waited hopefully for him to take hold again, and waited in vain.

Soon all the annoying sensations returned, and I began to feel a little seasickish from the infernal toss and pitch of the boat. The rain poured down in a torrent. Still I fished on, a most miserable wretch. As many and many a time before, I wondered what made me do this. What fettered me to this unhappy state? How utterly absurd and perfectly asinine this fishing game in such weather! I would certainly start back to camp presently, to warm fire, clothes, and supper; still I kept on fishing. I did not envy, any more than I could emulate, the myriad anglers who had recourse to strong hot whisky, but I at least understood them.

While crouching there I suddenly remembered Stevenson's *Lantern Bearers*, and my mind was illumined. The concrete fact of my actually being cold, wet, miserable had little to do with it. Only now and then was I conscious of such state. Like the little lantern bearers, boys at a game, sitting in the dark rainy night, with lighted bull's-eye lanterns hidden under their coats, I was almost oblivious to externals. The boy in me existed as always.

It was this then that nailed me to my martyrdom; this enchantment of the mind, this illusion. The shibboleth I might have cried out in the teeth of the rain was that I was fishing; that the fisherman is born, not made.

Five more days of rain and wind! Then came a change, or at least something to delude us. We went to the Cavalli Islands again, arriving about ten o'clock.

FROST FISH FOUND IN STOMACH OF BLACK MARLIN

PLATE LXX

THE SINGLE HOOK ADVOCATED BY ALL AMERICAN SPORTSMEN

PLATE LXXI

The aftermath of the storm was manifest in the huge swells piling up on the rocks and the unearthly roar of waters. We tried drifting around the islands. Not a strike in four hours! Then we ran outside to find schools of *kahawai* on the surface, and swordfish everywhere. Captain Mitchell caught two, and I caught three. They were jumpers with a vengeance; and in those great swells it was something unforgettable to see the pyrotechnics. I got upward of one hundred leaps out of mine. The last of my triplets was a "long lean hungry soaker," as Frank called him, that had a broken bill. His performance of forty-one leaps, of all kinds and heights, was a truly wonderful example of swordfish agility. He was hard to whip, too.

This particular Marlin had roused my curiosity long before he was lashed to the stern. If it had been possible I should have let him go alive. He had an extraordinary build, very long, slender, round, with a spread of tail large enough for a five-hundred-pound fish; but his beauty was marred by the absence of his bill. It had been broken or bitten off long before, no doubt in terrible encounter with rival or foe.

Deprived of his weapon of defense and for procuring food, this Marlin might well have been expected to be thin, flat, in poor condition. Nevertheless he was solid, fat, in splendid shape. He had been compelled to rely on his speed; and I surely could testify to that.

Another of my swordfish had a healed wound fully a foot long, back of the dorsal fin, where some huge shark had bitten out a piece. All these swordfish showed scars of battle, of the unremitting strife that goes on under the sea.

CHAPTER IX

WE HEARD from reliable authority that two large Marlin swordfish had been found dead some time ago along the beach of Whangaroa Harbor. No particular thought was given this, though the lengths of the fish were taken. The longest measured thirteen feet, eight inches; the other over thirteen feet. These fish were almost certainly black Marlin.

As to the exceeding great size I was not so astonished as thrilled. R. C. and I both had seen black Marlin off the White Friars in Mexican waters, that were close to fourteen feet in length. A more accurate estimate could not be made, as we sighted the Marlin back of our teasers and under the water. My opinion as to the size of these fish has been ridiculed in certain quarters. Captain Mitchell's capture of a twelve-foot, eight-inch black Marlin weighing nine hundred and seventy-six pounds is something of a vindication.

Now a great black Marlin a foot longer than the Captain's would be fully that much larger in girth, perhaps more. At the very least it would weigh three hundred

pounds more. Shades of fishes! Once more I am reminded of the twenty-five-foot sailfish off Madagascar in
the Indian Ocean. Always there will be bigger fish in
the sea than are ever caught!

Alma Baker kept importuning me to join him in taking
a trip to the North Cape, about eighty some miles up the
coast, where, the Maoris had informed him, there were
huge mako and swordfish, and a very game fish called
ahiriri, never yet caught on a rod. The Maoris caught
this fish on hand-lines, and claimed it jumped marvelously.

Captain Mitchell added his persuasion, and so, much
against my judgment, for we had located big fish and it
was not sense to leave them for mere possibilities, I consented to go, and we planned for about a five-day trip.
In the end Mr. Baker, on account of threatening weather,
decided to hold over awhile; but Captain and I went
ahead.

On the way up, off the Cavallis, I landed a fine striped
Marlin of three hundred and twenty pounds, and then
a mako, just one hundred pounds less in weight. Captain Mitchell began badly, losing three fish.

That afternoon late we ran into Whangaroa Harbor.
The entrance was narrow, between high walls; inside, a
wonderful bay opened out, having many picturesque
ramifications deep into the headlands. Dome-like peaks
towered over the bay. The slopes on many sides were
delicately green with tree ferns. Here and there deep
canyons ran down rugged and rough to the water. Sheer
perpendicular cliffs, yellow slopes, ragged walls of lava
and glistening beaches of sand surrounded this beautiful
many-bayed harbor. One little hamlet, consisting of a

few houses, located miles inland from the entrance of the harbor, kept it from being utterly lonely and wild.

The next day was bad. We ran thirty miles north, trolling baits all the way, without a strike. Captain Mitchell said he raised several Marlin that refused to bite. Off the Kara Kara Islands we were joined by Baker, who had come on and was keen to continue to North Cape. But I did not care to place any more miles of rough sea between me and the place where I knew I could raise fish. Baker went on, while Captain Mitchell and I turned back.

Late that afternoon, just off Cape Kara Kara, we saw some favorable indications of bait, so halted there to fish awhile. I saw two swordfish tails cutting the swells, for the sea was heavy, but could not follow them. A little later, just as I got fast to a hard-fighting yellowtail, the boatmen both sighted an enormous fin. They yelled, "Black Marlin!" And there I was tied up to a bulldog yellowtail. The swordfish swam along not far from us. I labored frantically to haul the yellowtail in, so we could hurry after the Marlin. Meanwhile it swam leisurely toward Captain Mitchell's boat. At last I freed my line of its heavy incumbrance, and we shot away in chase of the black Marlin. I was just in time to see that fish rush after Captain Mitchell's teasers. It refused his bait, but took one Bill let out on the second rod. There was a mix-up when Bill tried to hand the rod to Captain Mitchell. Between them they bungled the chance and missed the fish. Imagine my consternation, dismay, then bitter disappointment! All the rest of that fruitless day this last proof of my lucklessness rankled in my breast. I fought the morbid suggestion. No such thing as luck, good or bad! So I tried to delude myself. Vain oblation!

That sunset we cast anchor in a perfectly sheltered crescent bay, with wide sand beach and canyoned bluffs on one side, and red chalk hills on the other. Outside, the surge boomed on the rocks; inside, the wash of the waves on the strand was soft and musical. Sheep bleated on the far grassy slopes. In the notch between the mountains on the mainland the sun sank shrouded by the smoke of autumn fires. How the sweet smell of burning leaves made me thrill sadly and longingly for the autumn fields of lands far away and days long ago!

A hermit thrush, caroling his lonely twilight song, added poignantly to my feeling. Then I heard a strange bird note, most striking to me. It was the low sweet toll of a bell. I thought my ears had deceived me. But Morton, the New Zealander with me, told me the bird was the tui, a native songster of the island that imitated the real and rare bell bird. I listened for a long time, and at length was rewarded by another of the exquisitely clear and deeply sweet bell notes. But though I waited longer, no repetition came to my expectant ears.

Night found me weary and prone to the disenchantment of fishing. The motion of the boat was like a gently rocked cradle. My bed felt warm and snug. Outside, the haunting sounds of the sea and the distant clamoring of gulls filled my ears until they heard no more.

Before seven the next morning we were on our way back to the Cavallis, hopeful again, rested, full of eagerness for the long thirty-mile troll. But the morning calm was a delusion, the smooth sea a deceit, and the ever newly born hope of a fisherman without fruition. I trolled all day. Toward evening I raised a striped Marlin that was as cunning as an educated fox. He just wanted to play with the teasers. Captain Mitchell told me, when we again dropped anchor, that he had raised three swordfish just as tricky and wary as mine.

Morning broke dark, with lowering clouds, cool wind, and a redness in the eastern sky. "When it is red in the

morning, the sailors take warning!" goes the old saying.
Nevertheless we undaunted and once more hopeful anglers ran off to the Cavallis to fish.

In the first place, it took a long time to catch bait. In the second, the wind freshened, the sea came up to meet the swell that had persisted for days. We could not find any fish near the rocks or close offshore, so we ran out four or five miles. We trolled, then drifted, trolled and drifted again. Finally Captain Mitchell hooked something. We ran close to watch. It was a heavy fish. The big swells lifted the boat, making a fight with a fish straight down something most exasperating. Captain Mitchell broke his black palm rod. By hard work he and his boatmen maneuvered to get the line on another rod and reel. Then the Captain, feeling sure of the hickory, began to haul on that fish very hard indeed. I cautioned him twice; but in spite of my warning he broke the hickory square off at the reel seat. After that he and the men hand-lined up a five-hundred-pound reremai. Two rods broken on an old shark! The Captain looked what he felt.

That was catastrophe, but nothing to what befell me presently. We went on trolling, and after a while I saw a flash of purple color back of the left teaser. Jumping up, I espied a large Marlin shape rather deep down and dark in color. I yelled for the boatman to haul in the teasers. "Looks like a pretty big fish," shouted Frank.

Then the swordfish went for my bait. He did not show very distinctly, as he kept well under on a slant. He seized the bait and flashed away with inconceivable speed. I felt his weight before I put on the drag. He practically hooked himself. Like an arrow from a bow he sped ahead of us as if the drag was nothing. Then he sounded just as swiftly, and suddenly came up to leap half out. "Black Marlin!" we all yelled simultaneously. Then for a moment we gave way to elation.

Peter had been up on deck, standing, and he had the best look at the fish. "Between four and five hundred pounds," he said. I thought the fish would weigh more than that. Fish seen in the water always look smaller than they really are.

With sight of that black Marlin, and then the sudden tremendous strain on my rod, I was seized with wild exultation. I felt I had him solidly hooked. My sensations were thrilling in the extreme. Happy as a boy!

We ran along with the fish, and my line cut the water about fifty feet out. It appeared to curve toward the boat and to move faster. Suddenly the line whistled through the water. It was curving toward the bow, swift, swifter!

"Look out, Frank!" I yelled in alarm.

He threw on full speed just as my line shot squarely under the boat, high up on the surface. I had only time to throw off my drag and release my harness hooks. My line spun off my reel, then slacked. I felt it had caught on the propeller. Next I saw it trailing limp behind the boat. Catastrophe! I realized it with terrible intensity, but for an instant could not believe the evidence of my eyes. What a pang tore my breast! I was frantic in protest against such horrible sudden misfortune.

While I sank back in my chair, crushed, overcome, the boatmen drew in the line and disentangled it from the propeller. Almost a hundred yards was missing. Neither of them made any comment at first. As for me I went into the cabin and lay down, conscious of loss utterly out of proportion to the actual facts. It was only a fish! But the transition from sheer exultation to stark tragedy was too violent, too swift for me to bear with equanimity. Bad indeed were those few moments in the cabin.

Nor was that quite the end of an imperfect day! The southwest wind increased to a gale, and we had to buck it for eighteen miles to get back to camp. I was thoroughly used up, and bruised all over from the knocking about of the boat on the rough waters.

Ten years before this I had fought and lost the first black Marlin I ever saw, though I did not then know it under such name. This happened in Catalina waters. I never forgot that nine-hour battle. Then last winter I had my record encounter with one of these grand game fish. It lasted over four hours and ended in calamity. I had hooked three black Marlin in New Zealand waters, all of which had actually outwitted me. They appeared to be incredibly fast, strong, sudden and resourceful. Captain Mitchell averred that nothing but sheer luck saved both his fish. The larger black Marlin took all his line in one run, and stopped with only a few yards left on the reel. He testified to the bewildering suddenness of their change of tactics, though fortunately neither of his fish darted under the boat. If my boatman had deliberately kept far away from this last black Marlin I hooked, we might have caught it. But we could not foresee such an apparently impossible move. It taught me, most bitterly, that no skill on the part of angler and boatman was equal to the supremest sagacity and rapidity of this wonderful black Marlin.

We were fishing around Bird Rock a day or two afterward. The swells were mountainous; and to troll in such a sea was futile. Nevertheless we made the attempt and showed perseverance worthy of a better cause.

Illustrating the Three Types of Bill. Left—Broadbill Swordfish. Center—Black Marlin. Right—Striped Marlin

PLATE LXXII

TACKLE AND BAIT

PLATE LXXIII

Captain Mitchell took to drifting with live bait, and I followed suit. The change was restful, as the boat rode the long slow swells with ease and grace, and the motion grew exhilarating. After a time we saw a dark fin cutting the water close to the Captain's boat. His men saw it, for they waved with gestures of deprecation, meaning the fin belonged to a hammer-head. But really it belonged to a mako, which most assuredly showed its preying nature by charging my bait. I saw the fish in the top of a clear green swell, its sharp vicious nose, prominent eyes, strange bullet shape, green and gold, and the motion of a tiger on the spring.

This mako was the largest I had felt. He astonished me. His burst out of a swell, straight across the deep hollow into another swell, was something electrifying, and most beautiful to see. We were far behind time in trying to photograph him. But we made ready for a second jump. As he shot off with my line I knew neither Frank nor Peter would cover him with camera if again he leaped. Suddenly out he shot, not high, but low, straight across the sea in a long greyhound leap. My line went slack. Upon reeling it in I found my leader bitten off as cleanly as if it had been done by nippers.

"That was a big one. Four hundred!" Peter ejaculated. "Dod gast it! That fellow you wrote about, who said you were the most unlucky fisherman in the world, had it right-o!"

One other boat besides ours was fishing there; and it contained two boatmen who had no angler for the day and were fishing for themselves. Evidently they were enjoying it. When quite some distance away from us they hooked a fish, and proceeded to run out to sea. Presently they came back; and we did not need to be told they had lost it. I had seen this identical thing happen many times. As they passed us one of them yelled lustily, spreading wide his hands:

"Big black Marlin! He rolled up once; wide as a door!"

It was simply impossible for me to evade the shock that was equivalent to a hurt. The thought of another grand swordfish breaking away from that flimsy tackle, with a triple gang hook in its stomach, made me positively sick. How many times had that identical thing happened in the half dozen years of New Zealand swordfishing? Hundreds, no doubt! Not one of those large Marlin had ever been captured on the kind of tackle used, and not one ever would be. While succumbing to despair I could only hope that time would educate these anglers to the futility of such method.

That incident took the heart out of the afternoon, and I was glad when the sea grew so rough we had to quit. At camp Captain Mitchell expressed himself vigorously, and when he said, "What a pity you couldn't have had that strike!" I threw up my hands.

"Never mind, old man, you're going to get your black Marlin," he added feelingly.

That night the strong wind beat the flaps of my tent, the *ti* trees moaned, and the flags rustled. The tide surged in to the bank, low, sullen, full of strange melody. And it seemed to me that an old comrade, familiar, but absent for a long time, had returned to abide with me. His name was Resignation.

Daylight next morning disclosed gray scudding clouds and rough darkened water. We remained in camp and tried our hands at the many odd jobs needful to do but neglected. After a while the sun came out, and at noon the wind appeared to lag or lull. The thing to do was to go fish. I knew it, and I said so.

Out at Bird Rock we found conditions vastly better

than we had expected. The schools of bait, white and frothy, were working everywhere, with the sea gulls screaming over them. High swells were rolling in, but without a break or a crest. Four boats besides ours were riding them. The clouds had broken and scattered, letting a warm sun shine.

We trolled around the rock, to and fro past the churning foamy schools of *kahawai*, and out farther, long after the Captain had taken to drifting. At last we raised a large striped Marlin. He was so quick that he got hold of a teaser. That made him wary, and though he at last swam off with my bait, he soon let it go. After such treatment we took to drifting. Pretty soon Frank called:

"They're waving on the Captain's boat."

"Sure enough," I said. "Guess he must have a strike or have seen a fish."

But when Bill appeared waving the red flag most energetically I knew something was up. It took us only a moment or two to race over to the other boat, another one for me to leap aboard her, and another to run aft to the Captain.

His face was beaming. He held his rod low. The line ran slowly and freely off his reel.

"Got a black Marlin strike for you," he said with a smile. "He hit the bait, then went off easy. . . . Take the rod!"

I was almost paralyzed for the moment, in the grip of amaze at his incredible generosity and the irresistible temptation. How could I resist? "Good Heavens!" was all I could mumble as I took his rod and plumped into his seat. What a splendid, wonderful act of sportsmanship—of friendliness! I think he realized that I would be just as happy over the opportunity to fight and capture a great Black Marlin as if I had had the strike myself.

"Has he showed?" I asked breathlessly.

[115]

"Bill saw him," replied Captain.

"Hell of a buster!" ejaculated Bill.

Whereupon, with chills and thrills up my spine, I took a turn at the drag wheel and shut down with both gloved hands on the line. It grew tight. The rod curved. The strain lifted me. Out there a crash of water preceded a whirling splash. Then a short blunt beak, like the small end of a baseball-bat, stuck up, followed by the black-and-silver head of an enormous black Marlin. Ponderously he heaved. The water fell away in waves. His head, his stubby dorsal fin, angrily spread, his great broad deep shoulders climbed out in slow wags. Then he soused back sullenly and disappeared.

"Doc, he's a monster," exclaimed the Captain. "I sure am glad. I said you'd get fast to your black Marlin."

After the tremendous feel of him, and then the sight, almost appallingly beautiful, my uncertainty ceased. He was there, solid and heavy. Whereupon amid the flurry of excitement on board I settled down to work, to get the hang of the Captain's tackle, the strange chair and boat. None of these fitted me, and my harness did not fit the rod. But I had to make the best of it.

The swordfish headed out to sea, straight as an arrow, and though I pumped and reeled with fresh and powerful energy he gained line all the time. We had to run up on him so that I could get the line back. My procedure then was to use all the drag of reel and hands I dared apply. This checked him. He did not like it. Slowly the line rose, so slowly that we all knew when and where he would show on the surface, scarcely a hundred feet away. Frank and Peter, in my boat, were opposite, running along with us; and they were ready with cameras. Mitchell and Morton also had cameras in hand. What a long time that break was in coming! A black blunt bill first came out. Then with tremendous roar of water the fish seemed to slip up full length, a staggering shape of black opal, scintillating in the sunlight, so wide and deep and ponderous, so huge in every way, so suggestive of immeasurable strength that I quaked within, and trembled outwardly with a cumulation of all the thrills such moments had ever given me.

As he thumped back, sheets of green and white spread, and as he went under he made a curling swirl that left a hole in the water. Then he sounded, but he did not stay down long. That is one of the fine things about Marlin swordfishing. As he came up again at the end of that run, I had to have the help of the boat to recover two hundred yards of line.

The sun had come out hot. The seas were flattening. I began to sweat and burn, but never did an angler enjoy more such results of labor. This swordfish was slow. I could tell what his moves would be. Still, remembering the others that had fooled me, I did not trust him. With hawk eyes I watched the tight singing line. If it curved the least at the surface I saw and gauged accordingly.

When we ran close again it was evident that the black Marlin meant to rise and come out. How wonderful to see the line rise! To expect the leap and know for sure! We were all ready, with time to spare. Yells of various kinds greeted his glistening bulk, his great wagging head. He veritably crashed the water. And he rose so high that he lifted my line clear of the water, straight and tight from fish to rod, ten feet above the surface. That was a remarkable thing; and I did not remember it having happened to me before.

He led us out to sea, and in two miles he flung his immense gleaming body into the air ten times. Naturally this spectacular performance worked havoc with my emotions. Every time I saw him I grew a little more demented. No child ever desired anything more than I that beautiful black Marlin! It was an obsession. I wanted him, yet I gloried in his size, his beauty, his spirit, his power. I wanted him to be free, yet I wanted more to capture him. There was something so inexpressibly wild and grand in his leaps. He was full of grace, austere, as rhythmic as music, and every line of him seemed to express unquenchable spirit. He would die fighting for his freedom.

Whenever he showed himself that way I squared my shoulders and felt the muscles of Hercules. How little I suspected pride goes before a fall!

Again I maneuvered to work close to him, and this time saw the double line slip out of the water. That was an event we all hailed with a shout.

"How much double line?" I asked Captain.

"Only fifteen feet," he replied dubiously. "You see that line is short anyway. I couldn't spare more."

This was the beginning of the other side of the battle, the fearful, worrying, doubtful time that was to grow into misery. A great fight with a great fish rings all the gamut of the feelings.

Grimly I essayed to pump and reel that double line to my clutching thumbs. I got it almost to the tip of the rod. As the leader was only twenty feet long my black Marlin was close. I risked more, straining the rod, which bent like a willow.

"I see him," yelled somebody out forward. Captain Mitchell and Morton ran with their cameras.

Suddenly the double line swept down and my reel whirred. A quick wave heralded the rise of the swordfish.

"Look sharp!" I called warningly, as I released my drag.

As he had been slow, now he was swift. Out of a boiling hissing smash he climbed, scarce a hundred feet from the boat, and rose gloriously in the light, a black opal indeed, catching the fire of the sun. But he could not clear the water. He was too heavy. I saw his great short club bill, his huge gaping jaw, his large staring black eye, terrible to behold. My own voice dinned in my ears, but I never knew what words I used, if any. His descent was a plunge into a gulf, out of which he thundered again in spouting green and white, higher this time, wilder, with catapultic force—a sight too staggering for me ever to see clearly enough to describe adequately. But he left me weak. My legs, especially the right one, took on the queer wabbling, as if I had lost muscular control. If the sight of him was indescribable, then much more so were my sensations.

Tense we all were, waiting for another burst on the waters. But it did not come. My swordfish quickened his pace out to sea. Sight of him so close had acted as a powerful, even an intoxicating stimulant. Like a fiend I worked. Half an hour of this sobered and steadied me, while it certainly told upon my endurance. I had labored too violently. As many and many a time before, I had not kept back a reserve of strength.

Suddenly with a crack the reel came off the rod. My grasp of it kept it from going overboard. "Quick!" I yelled frantically. "The reel's come off. Help!"

The situation looked desperate. I released the drag, letting the swordfish free of strain. Fortunately he did not rush off. While Captain Mitchell bound the reel seat on the rod I performed the extremely difficult task of carrying on without a bungle.

Naturally, though, I lost confidence in the tackle. I could not trust it. I did not know how much I could pull; and that with a new trouble, a slow rolling swell which made it almost impossible for me to keep my seat in the chair, operated to help the fish and wear me out. It took time to conquer this, to get back what I had lost.

Then the reel broke off again. As I was holding it, more than the rod, I lost my balance and half fell into the cockpit. All seemed lost. Yet, like the fool I was, I would not give up, but stung my companions to quick and inspired tasks, and then got the reel fastened on again. And in a short time I had gained all the line lost. My spirits did not revive to any degree, but at least grim disaster left me for the moment.

In the next half hour, strange to relate, encouragement did rise out of the gloom; and I worked so well and so hard that I began to imagine I might whip this great fish yet. To that end I called for my boat to come round behind us, so Peter could board us with my big gaff, and Morton could go on board my boat with his motion-picture camera. This change was made easily enough, and with Peter beside me I felt still more hopeful. I knew from the feel of my back, however, that I had overdone it, and should ease up on the rod and patiently save myself. But this was impossible.

Then the reel broke off the third time. I almost pitched both reel and rod overboard; but Peter's calmness and his dexterous swift hands had cooling influence upon me.

"You could fight him better from our boat," said Peter.

Why had I not thought of that before? This boat was new to me; and the location of the chair, the distance to the gunwale, the fact that at some turns of the chair I had no support for my feet, made all my extreme exertion of no compelling avail. After a little more of it, I again called for my boat to run close.

I released the drag, and holding the rod up, with Peter holding me, I made the change into the *Alma G.* without mishap. And then in my own chair I fell to fighting that

AUTHOR WITH 68-POUND YELLOWTAIL (*Seriola dorsalis*). ERRONEOUSLY CALLED
KINGFISH IN NEW ZEALAND

PLATE LXXIV

CAPTAIN MITCHELL'S 80-POUND YELLOWTAIL

PLATE LXXV

swordfish as hard as I had fought him two hours before. He felt it too. Slowly his quick, free, tremendous moves lost something; what, it was hard to say. Eight times I got the double line over the reel, only to have it pulled away from me. Each time, of course, the end of the leader came out of the water. Bill, who had come on board my boat with the Captain, leaned over at last and grasped the leader.

"Careful," I warned. "One hand only. Don't break him off."

Twice Bill held momentarily to the leader, long enough to raise my fluctuating hopes.

Peter stood back of me, holding my chair. The tremendous weight of the swordfish, thrown against the rod-socket, pushed the chair round farther and farther.

"Mr. Grey," said Peter, "what you want on that fish is your big tackle. If you pull the leader up again I can slip your line through the swivel."

"By George—" I panted. "Peter—you're—the kind of boatman—I want around."

Fired by this sagacious idea, I strained rod, reel and line, and eventually drew the leader up a foot out of the water—two feet—three, when Bill grasped it, and Peter with swift careful fingers slipped my line through the swivel, knotted it, and then with flash of knife cut the Captain's line.

"By gad! That's great!" ejaculated Captain Mitchell. "You'll lick him now."

Everybody whooped, except me, as I hauled away with the big rod that had killed so many big fish. I seemed to have renewed strength—I certainly saw red for the moment and swore I would pull his head off. In short order I had the leader out of the water again, closer and closer, until Bill once more grasped it.

This time he held on. Frank kept the boat moving

ahead. We gained on the fish. Slowly he rose, a huge shining monster, rolling, plunging. My heart leaped to my throat. Bill yelled for help. Peter, with gaff in right hand, leaned over to take the leader in his left. I could see how both men strained every nerve and muscle. That frightened me. How many great fish had I seen lost at the boat! The swordfish pounded the water white just out of reach. I ordered the men to let go; and with a thumping splash he disappeared and took line rapidly.

He seemed a changed swordfish. He ran off much line, which was hard to get back. He grew wild and swift. He had got his head again. Perhaps the stronger tackle, the narrow escape at the boat, had alarmed him. Anyway, he was different. He kept us going. But I felt master now. I knew I could whip him. My aching arms and paining back were nothing. His long runs did not worry me. Let him drag three hundred yards of line! But when he got too much line we shot ahead so that I could recover it.

So that stage of the fight went on and neared the end. I felt that it would mean victory. There are signs a fisherman can detect, movements and sensations which betray a weakening fish. I kept my knowledge to myself. How many mistakes fishermen make!

This period was somewhat after the third hour. It had not afforded me much relief, although a restored equilibrium certainly helped. The next action of significance on the part of Mr. Black Marlin was to sound. He had not attempted this before to any extent, but now he went down. I made no effort to check him. Indeed, that would have been useless. I watched the line slide off, in jerks, yard by yard; and through my mind went many thoughts, all optimistic. When a great fish sounds after a long fight it is favorable to the angler. At the depth of five hundred feet the pressure of water is tre-

mendous, and the farther down then the greater pro-
portionately. Broadbill swordfish often sound with
their last flurry of departing strength.

My black Marlin continued to go down. I asked
Captain Mitchell if his record nine-hundred-and-seventy-
six-pound Marlin sounded like that.

"Yes, only not so deep; and earlier in the fight," responded the Captain. "I don't like the idea of this
fellow. He's getting too deep. Suppose he should die
down there?"

"Well, I reckon the old tackle will lift him," I replied
confidently.

Nevertheless Captain Mitchell's concern was trans-
ferred to me. It was too late to attempt more strain;
indeed I had to ease off the drag. Slowly and more
slowly sounded the swordfish, until he was taking inches
instead of feet. Then, at last, he stopped taking line altogether. One thousand feet down! There he seemed
anchored.

Hopefully I waited for some sign of his working back.
None came. Then I braced my shoulders, heaved on
my harness, and stretched my arms in a long hard lift.
The old rod described a curve, till it bent double and
the tip pointed straight down at the water. I waited for
the spring of the rod, for the slow rise of the tip that
always helped so materially to bring up a fish. The
spring came, but so slowly that I had more concern added
to my trouble. By dropping the rod quickly and swiftly
winding the reel I gained a few inches of line. This
action I repeated again and again, until sweat broke out
hot upon me. All the same a cold chill waved over my
back. I realized my gigantic task. The great swordfish
had fought to the last gasp, and had died down at that
tremendous depth. Now he was a dead weight, almost
impossible to move more than a few inches at each lift.

But still I felt perfect confidence in the tackle, and that by pushing myself to extremes I could bring this black Marlin up.

So I toiled as never before; and as I toiled all the conditions grew worse. It took both Captain Mitchell and Peter to hold my chair straight. The roll of the boat as it went down on a swell, added to the weight on the rod, pulled me from one side to the other, aggravating in the extreme.

Inch by inch! That old familiar amaze at myself and disgust at such senseless Herculean drudgery took possession of my mind. What emotions were possible that I had not already felt? I could not name any, but I was sure there were some, and presently I must suffer them.

When I timed a heave on the rod with the rise of the swell I managed to gain half a foot perhaps. If I missed the proper second then I failed to gain line. And as I lost strength the roll of the boat grew harder to bear. I was swung from one side to the other, often striking my knees hard. Then the chair whirled around so that I had no brace for my feet, in which case only the support of Captain Mitchell kept me in my seat at all. It grew to be torture that recalled my early fights with broadbills. Still I sweat and heaved and toiled on.

The moment arrived when I became aware that my rod was dead. It bent down to the water and did not spring up a fraction of an inch. The life of the great rod had departed on this giant black Marlin. If despair had not seized me, followed by a premonition of stark tragic loss, I would have been happy that this wonderful Murphy hickory rod—which had caught the world's record tuna, seven hundred and fifty-eight pounds and also six hundred and eighty-four, six hundred and thirty-nine, a host of other tuna up to three hundred and eighteen, nine broadbill swordfish and many Marlin—had bent its last on such a wonderful fish. But all I thought of was now I never could lift him!

Yet so intense was my purpose and longing that I found both spirit and endurance to lift him, inch by inch, more and more, until I knew that if I did not die myself, as dead as both rod and swordfish, I would get him.

All of a sudden Bill yelled out hoarsely and wildly: "My Gawd! look at that mako fin!"

We gazed in the direction indicated. As I was sitting down and hunched over my rod I was the last to see. The others, however, yelled, shouted and otherwise exclaimed in a way calculated to make one thrill.

"He's foolin' round that box of bait Peter chucked overboard," cried Frank.

"By gad!" ejaculated the Captain, breathing hard.

Then I saw at quite some distance the yellow box, and close to it a dark fin glistening in the sun, cutting the water swiftly, and so huge that I could not believe my eyes.

"Boys, that's no fin," I said. "That's the sail of a boat."

"Oh, he's a monster!" added Frank.

"Mr. Grey, that's the biggest mako fin I ever saw," said Peter, who was the only calm one of the lot.

"Captain, there's your chance. Go after him," I suggested forcibly.

"No. You need me here, Doc. We can't catch all the fish. A fish on the line is better than two in the water, you know."

"I don't need you," I protested. "I've got this black Marlin killed, and I can lift him. Take my other big tackle and go hand a bait to that mako. . . . Say, but isn't that some fin? Never saw one to compare with it."

Captain Mitchell still refused; and I actually had to drive him away from my chair. I yelled for the other boat to run close, and I saw that Peter put my other big tackle in Captain's hands.

"Good luck!" I shouted, as the boat sped away.

I could not forget my own fish, for the tremendous weight bore down upon my shoulders, but I just held on while I watched the Captain circle that mako. The big dark green fin disappeared and then showed again. I had a feeling of something tremendous about to happen.

The intervening distance was close to a quarter of a mile. I saw the boat circle the fin, get ahead of it, slow down. Captain Mitchell leaned far forward with his rod.

Suddenly the fin vanished.

"Somethin' doin'," yelled Frank, "and there'll be more in a minute."

It appeared to me that the Captain was jerked forward and lifted. I saw a low wide swift splash back of the boat. Next, the rod wagged most violently.

"Boys, he's hung that mako!" I shouted, with wild delight. Captain Mitchell's ambition to capture a great mako was second only to mine regarding the black Marlin.

"*There he is!*" shrieked Frank.

A huge long round gold-white fish pierced the sky. Up, up! He had not raised the slightest splash. Up he shot, then over in the air—a magnificent somersault, and down, slick as a trick diver.

The enormous size of the mako, even at that distance, could not be mistaken.

"Oh, Peter, he's big or am I seeing things?" I implored.

"Big? He sure is big. That mako will go over twelve hundred pounds."

As Peter ended, a cream-white torrent of water burst nearer to us, and out of it whirled the mako going up sidewise, then rolling, so his whole under side, white as snow, with the immense pectoral fins black against the horizon, shone clearly to my distended eyes. His terrific vigor, his astounding ability, were absolutely new in my experience with fish. Down he smashed into a green swell. We all heard the crash.

With bated breath we waited his next leap; but it did not come. When we turned our fearful gaze back to the boat we saw the Captain reeling in a limp line. The mako had shaken free or broken off. I sustained a shock then that I could liken only to several of my greatest tragic fishing moments.

The comments of my comrades were significant of their feeling.

"Well, Mr. Grey," continued the practical Peter, "you've got a fish here that'll take some landing."

That nailed me again to my martyrdom; and somewhat rested, or freshened by the intense excitement, I worked prodigiously, and to some purpose. Presently, when the pressure became overpowering, and I felt that something in me would burst, I asked Frank to throw in the clutch and start the boat very gently, to see if we could not break the swordfish from his anchorage. We were successful, but I did not want to risk it again. The next time that ponderous weight became fixed, immovable, I asked Peter to reach down with one hand and very carefully pull on my line, so as to start the fish again. This, too, was successful, without too great a risk. Once started, the fish came inch by inch until I gave out momentarily and he felt like an anchor.

The Captain's return to my boat was an event. He looked pretty agitated. Among other things he said: "Great Heavens! what a fish! I was terrified. It seemed that mako filled the whole sky. He was the most savage and powerful brute I ever saw, let alone had on a line!"

"Too bad! It makes me sick, Captain," I replied. "I never wanted anything so badly as to see you land that mako."

Then I went back to my galley-slave task again; and in half an hour had the great black Marlin up. Never shall I forget the bulk of him, the wonderful color, the grand lines. We had to tow him in.

Sunset was at hand when we passed Bird Rock, where the black Marlin had struck. The sea was smooth, rolling in slow swells, opalescent and gold. Gulls were sailing, floating, all around the rock, like snowflakes. Their plaintive sweet notes filled the air. Schools of *kahawai* were moving in dark patches across the shining waters. Cape Brett stood up bold and black against the rosy sky. Flocks of gannets were swooping in from the sea. In the west the purple clouds were gold rimmed above, silver edged below; and through the rifts burned the red-gold sun. I watched it sink behind the low cloud bank; and at the instant of setting, a glamour, an exquisite light, shaded and died. It was the end of day, of another of my ever-growing number of wonderful fishing days!

My black Marlin might have been a brother of either of Captain Mitchell's. He had great symmetry, though carrying his weight well back to his tail. His length was eleven feet, eight inches; his girth five feet, six inches; and the spread of his tail three inches short of four feet. Seven hundred and four pounds!

Three Hundred and Fifty-six pounds of Yellowtail

PLATE LXXVI

EIGHTY-TWO POUND YELLOWTAIL

PLATE LXXVII

CHAPTER X

SEVERAL times we had made preparations for a two-
day trip out to the Poor Knights, picturesque islands
twelve miles off the coast, but owing to high winds
and rough seas we were not able to go until the middle of
March.

Among the many Maori legends and stories we had
heard was one that concerned the Poor Knights Islands,
and which had made them renowned above other groups
of islands on this ragged shore of New Zealand.

In the early days, so history records, a tribe of two
hundred and fifty Maoris, men, women and children,
took refuge on the isolated and almost unscalable Poor
Knights. They had incurred the enmity of a large and
powerful tribe. It happened eventually that a camp fire
at night betrayed the whereabouts of the fugitives. They
were surrounded and captured, every last one of them,
and taken back to the mainland, to an encampment on
a beautiful sandy beach. Here a great festival or feast
was held, during which the captives were cooked and
eaten. Only one escaped the massacre, and that one

was a little child, a girl who had fallen or hidden under a pack during the frightful performance. She was saved, and lived to be a hundred and three years old.

Such a tale, grewsome as it was, could not but add to our interest in visiting the Poor Knights; and as luck would have it, the morning we started the sea was calm and smooth. From Cape Brett to the Poor Knights the distance was close to twenty-five miles. I sat or stood out on the bow of my boat during the whole of the three-hour run.

Slowly the dark islands rose out of the sea. Upon near view they were seen to be quite large, high, and with bright green domes above gray and yellow cliffs. The passageway between the two islands was dotted here and there with ragged jutting rocks. I was disappointed at the scarcity of birds and apparent absence of fish. At least we saw very little sign of bait or fish on the surface.

We trolled around the larger island, and while I fished I had opportunity to see the wonderful walls and heights at close range. These walls reminded me much of the canyon walls of Arizona, both in vivid hues and in the caverns, arches, shelves and bare blank space of rock. The sea had performed for these walls what the wind had worked upon the desert cliffs. How the surge rolled in, solemn and grand, to bellow into the black caves, or rise green and white and thundering against the grim walls! There was only one place where the heights were sur-mountable; and that was a narrow cove and steep crack, up which the doomed Maoris and their relentless pur-suers had climbed. On top there were heavily-timbered slopes and eminences, and no doubt many thicketed gorges where fresh water was available.

My impression of this larger island was of a wild and lonely fortress out in the ocean; and I imagined I espied the Maori scout who had seen the approach of the dreaded enemy. A few song birds that we saw and heard lent something softer to this forbidding yet beautiful rock. Patches of bronze grass contrasted vividly with copses of shining green. The presence of the sea seemed the most unforgettable thing. I could not rid myself of the haunting moan and boom of the sea.

I caught a mako and several large yellowtail. Captain Mitchell did not have any luck. Meanwhile the sky had become overcast and threatening. As there was no safe anchorage, we considered it wise to run for the mainland, and had not gotten far before a heavy squall burst upon us. Fortunately wind and sea were in our favor. The boatmen put up a sail, and that with the engine sent us along at record speed. It was fine to race over the green and white billows, with rain and spray beating in my face; to watch the sea birds skim the water, and the clouds over the mainland break to let silver rays and gleams shine through the mist.

We ran into the very bay that had become memorable through the massacre of the Maoris from the Poor Knights; and I walked along that wide curved beach, where they say skulls and bones are washed up out of the sand to this day.

Before that week ended Captain Mitchell and I had one of our remarkable experiences. A heavy run of Marlin swordfish came in to the cape, and we happened to be there before any other of the boats arrived. The day was pleasant, with rippling sea, smooth in the lee of the great rock. Several large patches of *kahawai* and *trevalli* were working to and fro, showing signs now and then of pursuers underneath.

The details of that day would be too bewildering to force upon any readers, even if they were ardent fishermen. Captain Mitchell had his best bag, catching five swordfish, two of which gave him hard hour-long fights.

He hooked one other Marlin which he lost, more by the fact of my being near than any awkwardness of his own.

Our two boats were rather close off the north point of the rock. Captain Mitchell, Peter and I all had strikes simultaneously, and all hooked our fish. They began to leap. I actually saw three large Marlin in the air between our boats at the same time. The Captain's fish ran round my line. Presently my Marlin leaped and tangled in his line. I released my drag, but Captain Mitchell did not release his, and as a consequence broke his line. He shook his fist at me, and I yelled back, "You should keep your fish away from mine!"

By noonday several other boats and yachts were on hand, full of enthusiastic anglers. Swordfish were striking everywhere. The schools of bait were on the run. I saw one man, fishing from a skiff, hook and lose two swordfish. Six other Marlin were hooked and lost from the two yachts. One other boat caught a fish during the several hours that I watched.

My own luck was remarkably mixed, good and bad, mostly bad. I actually hooked twelve swordfish, some of them over three hundred pounds. Four of these threw the hook at the first leaping run. Another I lost after nearly an hour's battle, and another let go of the hook before I struck. Two others came unhooked at the boat, after they had been whipped. I landed four. I was keen, of course, to beat Captain Mitchell, but it was just one of those days when the inexplicable happened. R. C. would have said, "Well, old top, you weren't shooting straight to-day," or else, recalling our baseball days, he would have said, "You're hitting off to-day. You're chopping at the fast curves, and pulling away from the plate!"

After the heat of battle and rivalry was over I was heartily glad I had lost most of my fish. Captain Mitch-

WORLD RECORD YELLOWTAIL, 111 POUNDS (Plates lxxviii to lxxix)
(*Caught by author on heavy tackle, this fish gave a remarkable exhibition.*)

PLATE LXXVIII

PLATE LXXIX

ell could be happy with his record. I would beat him next time. The other remarkable incidents in connection with this day were too many to remember or record. But I could never forget the way the Marlin flashed around my boat. We had two follow our lures when fishing for bait. I raised half a dozen Marlin with the teasers. We had two rise and take dead *kahawai* we had thrown away. I saw at least a dozen purple sickle tails stick out of the water. And lastly, Peter, fishing from the bow, had an enormous black Marlin follow his bait as he wound it in. Peter never uttered a sound at the moment. Later he told me that the fish was so huge it scared him. It swam round his dead bait and refused it, and then went down.

Upon returning to camp I greeted Captain Mitchell in this wise: "Cap, you sure shot your bolt to-day. If you had fallen overboard you would have hooked a Steinway piano. And now, with our last few days at hand, you'll be funny. You won't be able even to catch cold!"

Of course I was only joking, but as it chanced that is exactly what came to pass.

We had three days left, and among the many places to go, absolutely unfished waters, except by ourselves, I chose two that we had named The Groaners and Sunken Reef. The Groaners were some ragged low rocks, off one of the points, and Sunken Reef was a wide ledge about ten fathoms deep. These places were four miles apart, and not more than ten from a little cove on the mainland where we had a safe and quiet anchorage.

As it turned out we had scarcely any fishing at The Groaners, all of it being around and on Sunken Reef. I had discovered this reef by accident. Perhaps not wholly by accident, as several times the presence of gulls and schools of *trevalli* had made me wonder about this locality and spend some time there. While drifting I caught my hook on the reef, at less than ten fathoms. This was illuminating, and afforded my boatmen and me much satisfaction. Wherefore we hung around, while the Captain scoured the seas looking for that mako he wanted so badly.

I caught a forty-pound snapper on that reef, and several yellowtail. About the middle of the afternoon big fish came in to work on the school of *trevalli*. Then things began to happen. Before sunset I had several striped Marlin, one of which weighed three hundred and eighty pounds, the largest of that species I had ever seen. The Captain reported nothing but barren seas.

"Cap," I said, "you ought to follow me around more."

"By gad! I'd be afraid I'd swamp the boat," he replied. "But I had one wolloping strike to-day."

Next day I took Morton with me for the avowed purpose of having him take some pictures of my boat. But my real intent was to hook him on to a swordfish. He had never tried for big fish and was crazy to do so. I thought to do him a good turn and incidentally have some fun.

Indeed, as a man always experiences when he attempts a kindly act, I had more pleasure and reward than I had bargained for.

Trolling over Sunken Reef I raised a good big swordfish, and I hooked him solidly. Then, as he came up rather sluggishly and wallowed on the surface, I thought it a good chance to put Morton on the rod. I did so, and straightway the fun began. The fish woke up and began to run and leap, so that we were compelled to follow. Morton had no idea what to do with rod and reel, but was not slow to follow my instructions. At first he could do nothing at all with the Marlin, and his expression was one of mingled awe, dread and wild delight. Both my boatmen were hugely enjoying the situation; and I ob-

served that Frank ran the launch rather poorly for him.
When the swordfish sheered toward us and threatened
to ram the boat or leap into it, Morton was a spectacle
to behold. But whatever his feelings he was game; he
never spoke a word, and he worked valiantly with the
tackle. His shirt did not quite come off, as I have seen
happen with tenderfoot anglers, but it certainly came
up around his neck. He was red and sweaty. His
legs shook, and his left arm grew weak. I was afraid
he would not last the battle out, but he did; and when
we gaffed that swordfish I never saw a happier angler
novice. Morton was not a born fisherman, but he was a
made one.

About three o'clock the school of *trevalli* began to rise,
foam over the surface, crash the water white, and vanish
as if by magic. Big fish again! We trolled around without raising another with the teasers. We needed live
bait. The boatmen wanted to run way back to the
islands for live bait. "Nix," I said. "This bait is what
I want. Catch me a *trevalli*."

Frank vowed the *trevalli* would be too big. Peter
did not commit himself, though he was dubious. But I
knew. *Trevalli* could not be caught with a lure, so we
had to run around the school and snag one. It was fully
six or seven pounds, rather long in shape, oval and thin,
and bright silver—a very pretty fish. Once on the hook
it proved to be an ideal bait, apparently none the worse
for its predicament. Very soon I had a running strike.
The next few minutes we were trying to catch up with
a marvelously leaping striped Marlin, and while my companions essayed to photograph him in action, I was hard
put to it to keep him from getting away. I was an hour
on this splendid fish, again the largest I had ever seen
of his species.

We returned thrillingly to our Sunken Reef, to find

conditions there more and more fishy. Soon I had another *trevalli* on for bait, and hardly had Frank stopped the engine when I had another great strike.

I saw my line sweep out swiftly and rise toward the surface. Then the bulge of a big fish! I clapped on my drag. What a jerk! I was almost dragged over the gunwale. That fellow hooked himself and at once broke water in a wide-flung splash, disclosing great breadth of shoulder and great depth. But for the long rapier-like bill I would have mistaken him for a black Marlin. He tore off line out to sea, and kept us guessing. After a while he leaped, a wonderful series of leaps, all low and heavy, which did not disclose his size. But I had that pretty well figured, and worked as if I had tied up with one of the black fellows. Not easy to land was that striped swordfish! I had all I wanted for a quick violent fight.

It took the four of us to load him on the boat, a most gorgeous specimen of the striped Marlin; bronze-backed, silver-bellied, wide and deep and long, with vivid purple bands. He measured eleven feet, five inches in length, and four feet, two inches in girth. Even before getting these remarkable measurements I knew I had the world record for the striped Marlin. I knew he would exceed even the disqualified four-hundred-and-thirty and three-hundred-and-seventy-two pound Marlin taken in Catalina waters. My brother held the qualified record with three hundred and fifty-four pounds. "Well, old R. C.," I exclaimed, "I've surely got you trimmed."

As a matter of fact this beautiful Marlin weighed four hundred and fifty pounds.

Back at Sunken Reef, just before sunset, we had a hard time catching another *trevalli*. They had grown wary. Big game fish were chasing them up and down. Then at last when I did get a *trevalli* it was a large one—

too large I feared. Nevertheless some great game fish, probably a mako or a huge black Marlin, jerked it off my hook before I could wink. What a tremendous strike! I was stunned. The bait had been hooked on securely. Only a fish with large powerful jaws could have snapped him off without taking line.

That was the end of fishing for that day at Sunken Reef. We could not catch another *kahawai*, though we tried till dark. When we left, the school of *trevalli* were making white patches of foam on the black waters. Captain Mitchell's bad luck had prevailed. Nothing! Two more heavy strikes that took his baits were all he reported.

Our last day dawned calm, rosy, with quiet sea. This morning, after we had amply photographed and weighed the Marlin, I insisted that Captain Mitchell go with us to Sunken Reef.

"I want to end this trip right there," I added.

So we went together, caught our bait, and trolled out to sea. On the way to Sunken Reef I had a single leap out of another big striped Marlin. This inclined me to the opinion that a run of larger fish had come in, and the more I weighed the evidence the surer I was of it.

The sea was level and glassy. This was the fourth day without wind. Gulls, like white bits of cork, were floating all over the ocean. No sign of our school of *trevalli*. We trolled over Sunken Reef, and raised one swordfish that would not bite. That was number eighty-one to be raised by the teasers. We ran out to sea, and back in, and then we drifted for a time. No fish! After lunch we tried again, keeping the while a close watch on the gulls. It looked as if our last day was going to be unavailing, so far as fish were concerned. Finally we returned to Sunken Reef to find the *trevalli* working on the surface. We had several live baits which we proceeded to try.

My first strike resulted in a forty-pound yellowtail. When Peter hooked a larger one it gave him a tough battle in that ten-fathom water. Frank had immense glee in his brother boatman's vain efforts to subdue the fish. I was amused at their naïve remarks, especially when the fish escaped.

Presently I had a running strike that I took to come from a swordfish. But the fish sounded deep, and before very long I recognized the telltale tug and jerk peculiar to the yellowtail. Moreover, he was mightily heavy and powerful. I tried to fetch him up, but failed, much to the delight of both boatmen.

"That's another big kingie," averred Peter.

I tried a number of times to haul this stubborn yellowtail up, and, failing, had to settle down to a real earnest fight that lasted three-quarters of an hour.

"Oh, what a corker!" yelled Frank, as at last I brought the fish alongside.

"Beats the one-hundred-and-ten-pound record," added Peter, with much satisfaction.

Not proof against such remarks, I stood and looked over the side of the boat, while Frank pulled on the leader. The calm clear water afforded perfect vision. I saw a big fish head, broad, dark, with gaping mouth like that of a tuna. Then he rolled over on the surface, disclosing what seemed an impossibly large yellow tail. But how beautiful! Gold-tailed, green-backed, with the wonderful mother-of-pearl tints on the broad side, he was verily a magnificent fish. I thought of Hooper and Murphy, famous Avalon anglers, now dead and gone, who fished many years for yellowtail and considered it to be the equal of tuna. Next I thought gleefully of how thoroughly I had Captain Mitchell's eighty-pounder beaten. A little consolation was coming to me late!

This yellowtail, called kingfish by New Zealanders,

was their favorite fish before Marlin were known. It was while fishing for kingfish that an angler accidentally hooked a Marlin. This misnamed fish attains immense size in these waters. In the Gulf of California the yellowtail grows to seventy-five pounds or more in weight, though I have no record of any caught. Mine weighed one hundred and eleven pounds, beating the world record by a narrow margin of one pound.

Captain Mitchell had hovered around Sunken Reef. But it appeared to me he was using dead bait, to his disadvantage. I was to find out presently, however, that live bait could be most extraordinarily hard to catch. The school of *trevalli* appeared only at infrequent intervals, and then to remain on the surface just long enough for some enormous fish underneath to make them flash into a roar of seething waters and vanish.

The little white sea gulls, in flocks of thousands, screamed and screeched their own protests at this summary disregard of their needs. They had to eat also, and their meals depended upon the *trevalli* chasing the tiny minnows to the surface. But now the *trevalli* were concerned with the matter of self-preservation.

We saw a colossal *reremai* fin on the surface, weaving behind the *trevalli*. And poor unlucky Captain Mitchell had the terribly bad luck to have that shark take his bait. By strenuous labor he got the leader to Bill, who promptly looped it round the bit. That relieved the Captain of this unwelcome weight, and also half of his leader.

During the next hour, while I unavailingly essayed to catch a live *trevalli*, I saw Captain Mitchell catch two small mako, which he handled as if extremely annoyed at getting fast to them at that important hour.

Suddenly I heard a *plop*. Then I saw a yard-wide round back that I thought belonged to a porpoise. Only it did not! A long dark-bladed tail swept up. Black Marlin! My yell roused the boatmen. We were too late, however, as the giant fish passed our boat scarcely thirty feet away. We followed him, saw him several times, lost him, found him again half a mile from Sunken Reef, and got a bait and the teasers in front of him. I went through all the familiar thrilling agonies, augmented by the possibility of a marvelous climax for this last day. But the black Marlin would not rise.

We went back to Sunken Reef. There we saw Captain Mitchell wildly running about, and when we got within hailing distance, Bill yelled, "We had hold of a big black Marlin. Threw the hook!"

At that I lost my intense eagerness and insistent breast-convulsing excitement. I realized there was not to be any climax. The wonderful last day had ended, as far as catching fish was concerned. Still I went on fishing, trying to catch a live bait, trolling a dead one, drifting also, and to no avail.

The sun began to redden between the purple clouds above the purple ranges. We had a long run to make back to camp. The day was done. I suffered one shock, one twinge, and conquered that inexplicable desire to keep on fishing. Slowly I reeled in my line, and peace came to me.

Peace with the realization of many things: of the marvelous success of this New Zealand fishing; of the delight in virgin waters; of the desire and determination to come back, to fetch R. C. and my son Romer; to fetch my ship the *Fisherman*, and fish these waters right! What a prospect! I think it was decided then and there. It saved me wholly from anything but gratitude and appreciation. I concentrated all my faculties for a few intense absorbing moments of seeing, hearing, feeling.

There gloomed the broad dark sea. The swells were

slow and low, and a gentle ripple ruffled the waters. The white gulls, like showers of feathers, were now rosy in the sunset glow. They ascended to fly over the frothy patch of water where the *trevalli* roared like a running brook, and screaming they alighted amidst the school. Suddenly the *trevalli* raised a splash and disappeared, only to reappear. The birds took to wing again. The air was full of moving fluttering specks of white. Crash! Another great swordfish had smashed at the school.

To make this scene perfect for me, and no doubt for the Captain also, a gigantic black Marlin rolled up to show a long dark straight fin, broad as a board. He went down. Then the acre of *trevalli*, a creeping acre of white seething foam, burst into a crashing splash. It vanished like magic. I watched and listened. No doubt the little gulls were doing the same. Behind me I heard the soft gurgling sound of water. The *trevalli* had come up again. Then the gurgle increased to a distinct roar, loud as that made by a tumbling stream. Then crash!

The battle went on there over Sunken Reef. It was life and death, something vital, beautiful, inevitable and unquenchable, and at the same time sinister and tragic. The black mystic waters rolled over this hidden reef and the inexplicable nature of the deep. My moments of watching and listening lengthened until the sun sank in magenta haze over the ranges. Then as we sped away over the darkening sea, campward bound, with the last great day done, I watched the white gulls hovering and wheeling in the strange afterglow of light.

CHAPTER XI

WE ARRIVED at last at the termination of our
salt-water fishing trip and faced our journey inland, most of which was to be devoted to the
waters of the North Island of New Zealand.

All the privileges and courtesies imaginable were ac-
corded us by government and railway officials, which
added indeed to our comfort and pleasure.

We left Auckland one evening early and got off the
train at a way station sometime near midnight; and then
rode in a motor car through moonlit country, arriving at
length at a hostel in the wilderness. This was to enable
us to visit next morning the celebrated Waitomo limestone caves on the way to Rotorua.

I did not anticipate much in comparison with the great
caverns I had seen, especially the Caves of Bellamar in
Cuba, and the Mammoth Cave of Kentucky. In the
Waitomo glowworm cave, however, I was to find something vastly different, most unique, and strangely beautiful in the extreme.

We were led into a tunnel under a hill, down through

limestone halls and corridors to a subterranean river, and eventually to a dark "Stygian cave forlorn," the roof of which was studded with myriad tiny blue-white lights, like wan stars in a velvet-black heaven. From the obscure silent river shone a perfect reflection of these glowworm lights. Silence was imperative, so the guide assured us, as noise had an unfavorable influence on the glowworms, causing them to lose their brilliance.

We embarked in a flatboat and were taken some distance through the cave to a point where ebony night reigned, and yet was strangely illumined by the phosphorescent glow of the worms. How hard to believe that these lights were made by live creatures, in the interest of their self-preservation! Yet such was a fact. The realization of such knowledge was as striking as the sight of the lights. We might have been in the very bowels of the earth. We could not see each other, though we could see the pale lanterns of the glowworms. How weird and marvelously beautiful!

Upon returning, the guide flashed his light upon a close overhanging ledge, from which there appeared to hang a thick long fringe of delicate tiny silver beads, like drops of sparkling dew caught upon a spider web. Each glowworm let down a trap, as it were, with which he caught his prey. His light operated as a magnet to attract the fluttering moth or gnat that had wandered into the cave where the river entered. I watched until I saw two tiny insects caught on this delusive fringe. The glowworm had power to feel or see his prey, and draw it up.

To me this was another manifestation of the inscrutable and wonderful ways of nature. Indeed, how staggering to the thoughtful mind! Who could ever have thought of such a creature, dwelling in such a place, existing by such means? I left the glowworm cave, the richer for a very unusual experience and an added knowledge of nature and life.

That same day we motored on to Rotorua, finding the hundred and some miles most beneficial and soothing to eyes for weeks used to the glare of sea. The green hills and vales, the ferny dells, the green meadows—how my eyes seemed to drink them in! Most of the road was good, but some of it was bad, and as there had been rain we were delayed, and did not reach Rotorua until dark.

That night we were piloted to a Maori concert. This was my first contact with the Maoris. I had read and heard a great deal about these people, but had not been interested, except in the very interesting fact to me that the Maoris were extraordinary fishermen. Perhaps I had unknowingly classed the Maoris with South Sea races, such as the Marquesans and Samoans, and therefore was somewhat prejudiced. I was to experience an astounding surprise.

The audience, quite a large one of tourists and travelers, was first greeted by Mrs. Staples Brown, a Maori woman of distinction, who had married an Englishman and resided in London. Her talk was by way of an enlightenment to me. That was followed by introductory remarks from Dr. Buck, an educated Maori. He first introduced the chief Mita, who in his native costume made a striking and picturesque appearance. The chief, in most forceful voice and dignified manner, began his address, the content of which was translated by Dr. Buck. It consisted in greetings and salutations to the audience.

What was my amaze and embarrassment presently to hear Dr. Buck announce: "Greetings and salutations to Zane Grey, who has come from far to conquer the leviathans of the deep. We wish to bestow upon him the name Maui, after our Maui legend of the great fisherman of the Maoris."

[144]

Following my surprise came a feeling of genuine pleasure and appreciation. I bowed my acknowledgment to the speaker, and mentally vowed that I must learn the Maori legend of Maui.

At the conclusion of the chief's address Dr. Buck announced and explained the various songs and dances to follow. I could not recall when I had listened to such sweet singing as that of the Maori girls. It impressed me deeply. Classical music, except some of the great and familiar masterpieces, has never appealed to me. The Maori love-songs, as the interpreter called them, were wild and sad and wonderfully melodious; and when the girls repeated the chorus in English the effect was enhanced. I left there with my mind haunted by those rhythmic chords, and for me to remember a melody is extraordinary.

Next day the famous guide Rangi, a handsome Maori girl, piloted us through the valley of geysers and mud pits, and the *pa*, a Maori fort and village on an eminence, and to all the places of interest. Conspicuous among these was the Maori *whare puni*, or meeting house, with its wonderful carvings in wood, one of which represented a fish caught by the great fisherman whose name had been bestowed upon me.

Captain Mitchell scraped acquaintance with various anglers staying at the hotel, most of whom were from England. The lakes around Rotorua abounded with trout, and we were advised to linger and try our luck. We could not, however, get any satisfactory evidence as to the fly fishing.

On the following morning we visited Fairy Spring. It was not felicitously named, because it is a wonderful pool full of rainbow trout, instead of fairies. I have seen larger springs, notably the head of Oak Creek in Arizona, and a magnificent acre-wide bubbling well in the Flattop Mountains of Colorado; but I never saw such crystal-clear water as that in Fairy Spring. It was round, some thirty feet across, and very deep. The water boiled up from the sandy depths, and it was so clear that in some lights it did not appear at all like water. There were perhaps two hundred rainbow trout there, of all sizes from ten pounds down. They would eat out of your hands, yet were perfectly free to come and go as they chose. The outlet to the lake was some distance away. We were informed that at times there were five hundred trout in the spring. Captain Mitchell and I spent a long lingering hour watching those rainbows. Fairy Spring was a thing I wanted to take home with me.

After that visit we rode out into what is called the bush, but which we found to be forest country. We passed five lakes, all gems of blue set in emerald hills, and the last of which, about twenty miles from Rotorua, was especially beautiful. Here we had the pleasure of meeting two gentlemen anglers with whom Captain Mitchell had gotten acquainted at the hotel. They had not caught any fish. We watched them casting with the long unwieldy English salmon rods, to my mind much too heavy for trout, and did not see them raise a fish. Finally they gave up casting with fly, and came ashore to the launch, where they proceeded to rig up different tackles. I took the opportunity to watch them while the Captain talked. They rigged up fourteen-foot stiff rods they called spinning rods; and used as lures a spinner with triple hooks and an imitation minnow with two sets of triple hooks. Then they ran out across the lake. It was rather late in the day, nearly four o'clock, and I wondered what luck they would have.

That night, just about sunset, they returned to the hotel at Rotorua with nine big rainbow trout, the largest just short of ten pounds. It struck me that they had not required much time to catch those fish. So much for the heavy rods and artificial baits with triple hooks!

From Rotorua we motored on to Wairakei, a most beautiful resort, set down amidst huge pine trees the seedlings of which had come from my own country. Impossible to believe that a pine three feet at the base had grown so large in thirty-five years! Yet it was true. The color and fragrance of these trees, the sough of wind in their branches, shot me through and through with homesickness. I walked a long time alone down a spreading aisle; and my reflections were that Ulysses would have been happier had he stayed at home.

Alma Baker and his family welcomed us to this comfortable and delightful place. And that afternoon accompanied us to another valley of thermal wonders, quite different from those of Rotorua, and in my opinion much more interesting. One green hole of hot water especially fascinated me and roused my credulity. It was a different kind of geyser. Every four and a half minutes, by the watch, this circular dark-green deep pool became violently agitated. You heard a roar, then saw a wave. Next the water rushed up in a maelstrom-like whirl, hissing, steaming, at last to burst up into great spouts and flood out of the hole into the stream. It was most peculiar.

That night we went to see what is called the Blow Hole. The noise it made prepared me for something out of the ordinary. It was a vast volume of hot dry steam blowing with tremendous blast out from under a bluff of rock. My strongest impression was that under the crust of beautiful and picturesque New Zealand there were active volcanic forces, too powerful for a comfortable forgetfulness of the furnace nature of the bowels of the earth.

From there we went to see the falls of the Waikato

River by night. You cross a bridge over a narrow deep gorge through which roars this enormous volume of water. Colored lights thrown upon the long slant of rushing water and the huge billows of foam, and then on the falls where the river takes a splendid leap, were as lovely as imagination could picture. The thunder of the falls was deafening. The solid rock upon which I stood seemed to quake. A fine rainy mist wet my face. Great waterfalls by night are obscure and illusive. Your ear is filled with a tremendousness that your eye fails to grasp. You are drawn near the brink, which is terrifying. You shudder at the thought of a misstep, yet are incomprehensibly drawn to the very verge.

When daylight came next day it showed dismal low clouds and gusty flurries of cold rain. We motored on to Taupo, a hamlet on the shore of the great lake, where the Waikato River has its source. We found accommodation for one night only. All the hotels were full, or expecting to be, over the Easter holiday. Fishermen appeared everywhere in evidence. I saw a long porch lined with rubber boots, waders, hobnailed shoes, landing nets, etc. I could not see much of the lake for the rain and low clouds. What I did see was white-crested and angry, almost like the sea in a storm.

Here we were met by Mr. Wiffin, the government official who had charge of this part of our trip, and a native guide named Ricket. What I wanted in the way of a camp site appeared to be almost impossible to find on Lake Taupo. We decided at length to go to the mouth of the Waihora River in Western Bay, where we were certain to be alone. Wiffin was grim about that and Ricket rather non-committal. I pinned the latter down to answering some specific questions. He could not reply to my satisfaction, but there seemed nothing else to do except go. I did not like the prospect, nor did Cap-

CAPTAIN MITCHELL'S BLACK MARLIN, 976 POUNDS (Plates lxxx to lxxxv)
(World record for all species of fish caught on rod and line.)
PLATE LXXX

Plate LXXXI

PLATE LXXXII

PLATE LXXXIII

PLATE LXXXIV

PLATE LXXXV

tain Mitchell. Baker went back to Wairakei, saying he would come when we had found things to our liking and sent for him.

That night at the hotel we heard enough to daunt most any angler. The weather was bad. Few trout were being caught; only one that day! And none of late had been caught on the fly, so far as we could ascertain. Most anglers trolled the lake in launches. Ricket claimed night fishing was the only way to get results. Such fly fishing as the Captain and I were used to in Canada and Oregon was not possible in New Zealand, except when the trout were running up the Tongariro River, or some other swift tributary of the lake. We hoped to try the great Tongariro later, but for the present we wanted another and a lonely river, with conditions more or less to our liking.

We went to bed discouraged and dismayed. I lay awake a long time trying to get warm, while the wind and rain stormed at my window. Finally I went to sleep, and when I awoke in the morning the rain had ceased, though the sky was overcast and the cold wind persisted. It looked like a bad day to cross a lake noted for its freak conformation, its crater origin, its eccentricities, one of which especially was a propensity to raise rough water on sudden order. Nevertheless, as there were no hotel accommodations to be had, we decided to risk going.

By nine o'clock all our baggage and camp duffle, with ourselves, was on two launches at the river wharf, near the lake. Here was the source of the swift deep Waikato, surely one of the remarkable rivers of the world, and certainly one of the most dangerous. The water at considerable depth was a crystal green, almost transparent, and very deceptive. Also it was as cold as ice. A breeze whipped down the lake from the west, roughening up whitecaps in the distance.

The high shores and the mountains, beyond the wide bay near Taupo, still were obscured in gray forbidding clouds, so that I had no view of the lake and surroundings. We had fifteen miles to travel against an unfavorable wind. It did not hamper us, or occasion any uneasiness, however, until we passed the jutting cape six or seven miles from Taupo and turned west in to the deep indentation called Western Bay. I made out gray beetling cliffs, rising sheer from the lake, and dark ranges beyond.

We were well out into the lake when both wind and sea rose suddenly. The boat we were aboard was a diving duck if I ever saw one. It pitched into every wave, and the water flew over from bow to stern. We were heavily laden, with eight passengers and much luggage, so heavily that I feared to trust the boat in a following sea, otherwise would have turned back. Then instead of turning into Western Bay we had to head into the wind clear across that end of the lake. There was an hour when my concern was considerable, particularly as we had lost sight of the other boat, which contained most of our outfit. Two boats, as well as two hunters, should always stick close together. I ventured to tell this to the skipper, but it had no appreciable effect. The wisdom of my advice probably struck him next day, though he never admitted it to me.

Not until we were well under the western headland did I relax vigilance or anxiety. Then in water growing calm and safe I began to take some notice of the lake shores. Gray clouds had broken, letting some sunlight through, and glimpses of blue sky.

As we neared the shore line I made it out to be gray cliffs, like colossal walls, overgrown with green. The rim was almost level and was high, in some places a thousand feet above the lake. Breaks in this wall were mouths of canyons, out of which flowed the Waihaha and Waihora Rivers. The curve of Western Bay covered miles in extent, on the west side stretching away to the cloud-obscured mountains. Presently I could see a long crescent beach, with a dark gap under the north wall, where the river broke through the sand bar. Back of the beach a dense green of foliage contrasted markedly with the drab walls. Despite the dull daylight and the absence of color the prospect was beautiful. A quarter of a mile from shore the water shoaled to twenty feet, through which the ribbed sand, level as a floor, showed as in a mirror. We ran the launch bow first upon the sand, and while the baggage was unloaded I searched for a camp site.

To my dismay I found the whole place on the left of the little river dug up and plowed over by wild pigs. There was no suitable place to pitch our tents. My dreams of a beautiful green and shaded bank above a rushing many-stoned white-pebbled river, where the trout flashed in the sunset, faded away as so many of my dreams have faded. According to Ricket this spot was the only one on the western side of the lake. Maoris lived at the mouth of the Waihaha. So I had to swallow my disappointment and make the best of a bad bargain. It cheered me a little to see the other boat coming; and later, by wading the icy river, I found a more desirable place for our personal tents. We had to pitch the cook tents on the side where the pigs had rooted so prodigiously.

Then there was work for everybody, with a lot left over. Darkness found us in fair shape for a comfortable night, and when supper was ready we ate in the dark, under a fly upon which the rain pattered. That night I slept like a log.

I was awakened by the song of birds. Strange deep bell-like notes, a metallic clink, a lonely plaintive single sound repeated at intervals, and a sweet twittering chorus greeted my ears. I listened with growing pleasure. Every note was new to me, and the wildness exquisitely marked. Here indeed was some reward for such a journey. Keen was I to make the acquaintance of these wild birds of a far-away land.

Upon arising I had a second and greater surprise. The sun was up somewhere, though not in sight; the lake shore was like a sheet of dark glass; the great dark walls curved away on each side, and across Western Bay, above the bold shore line on that side, rose a magnificent snow-capped mountain, and beside it, still higher, the black cone peak of a volcano, from which the white smoke rolled. I was transfixed. The scene was strikingly different from any I had recorded; and it had some quality I could not at once grasp. Beauty was not wanting, but that did not seem to be the dominant note. Sublimity was there, but it was not that. I realized I would have to study it out.

Then I made a discovery that I was sure would lead to a full appreciation in time. Lake Taupo lay in a vast crater, the sheer walls of which could be seen plainly on all sides across the lake twenty miles distant. And beyond them stood up the dark ranges that wandered away back of the great peaks. I was slow to remember that I had been bitterly disappointed. The fact was I had conceived impressions too quickly. On the other hand I was now quickly appreciative of the wonder and strangeness of this volcanic country. It awed me. Here was as much to see and learn as I had ever found in any other place. I was still watching when the sun came up over the rim of the eastern wall and made the lake a reach of diamond ripples, and the shore line a vast belt of soft gray. The white peak with the sharp black cone towered majestically against the blue sky.

CHAPTER XII.

AFTER breakfast Captain Mitchell and I took our rods and started up the Waihoro River, our hopes high with that old boyish eagerness peculiar to fishermen.

A couple of hours later I might well have said that all we achieved was a start. We did, however, get a little way, through a jungle of ferns and brambles. Often I have written of the impenetrable nature of rhododendron thickets, the stubbornness of manzanita copses, the matted web of scrub oak; but this jungle had them beaten altogether. The ferns were higher than our heads, laced inextricably, and plentifully strengthened and fortified with a kind of bramble that made cactus appear gentle. This bramble had a curved cat claw that reached for you, stuck deep and held fast. But such was the persistence of the Captain and myself that we kept on, encouraged or at least held to our purpose by occasional encroachments upon the river bank and the sight of a huge trout.

Captain Mitchell can cast a fly straight up and then

cast it out. But not I! I never got my fly even wet. Some of the holes were marvelous to look into. Deep, a light green, like aquamarine, with white sand bottom, against which background the huge brown and rainbow trout showed as clear as cameos. Also these holes were festooned around the shores by roots and snags, making it impossible to land a fish had we hooked one. Yet remarkable to state, we fished on. Those pools were irresistible.

At length we discovered a log lying across the stream, somewhat under the water, and we waded over on that, hoping to find less impassable jungle, through which we could progress by following the wild-pig trails and tunnels.

I lost sight of Captain Mitchell presently, but soon afterward I heard him. He fell off a bank into shallow water. I yelled, "Cap, are you drowned!"

"No," he shouted, "I'm all right. . . . By gad! there's a wolloping trout here!"

Whereupon I passed by upstream and got lost. I could not find the river or the way back. I was caught in a sort of uncanny thicket, gloomy and hard; and the crisscross of wild-pig tracks reminded me of the javelin tracks in the jungle of Mexico. At last I gave up my insane purpose to push on to find a fishing hole, and tried to retrace my steps. I only got in worse.

I came, finally, to a dense thicket through which I crawled on hands and knees on a broad pig trail that penetrated it. This trail led through another matted growth of ferns. Grimly I ambled along, finding no end of difficulty with my rod. The line was always catching. Suddenly I happened to think: "Suppose I come face to face with one of these wild boars Ricket advised us to avoid."

The thought made me uneasy, and I hurried. Suddenly a crash of brush ahead of me occasioned me more than disquietude. I stopped. I heard quick thuds. Then a huge yellow pig, a vicious long-snouted boar, came face to face with me, not twenty feet away! Even at the first glance I noticed he did not have any tusks; but he looked bad. I was so scared that I became facetious.

"Excuse me, Mr. Wild Boar," I said. "I have not the slightest intention of disputing your right to this trail."

Then when I was about to plunge into the brush the boar gave a great grunt and forestalled me. He piled into the thicket, making a great racket. I heard him thump over a bank and souse into water. Next came a wild yell from Captain Mitchell. The boar had evidently plunged down upon the Captain's fishing covert. I yelled: "Look out, Cap. It's a rhinoceros!"

Splashings and crashings acquainted me with the manifest desire of both the Captain and the boar to put distance between them.

I got back to camp first, hot and peeved, torn and dirty, yet somehow amused at the idea of fishing the Waihoro River. It was only a little brook, in spite of the deep pools. And they could not be fished from an airplane.

When finally Captain Mitchell arrived he was so much wetter and dirtier and angrier than I had been, that I at once saw the humor of the incident, and had a great laugh.

"Did you see that wild boar?" he queried with a stare.

"See him! Say, Cap, I met him in a hand-to-hand encounter, almost."

"By gad! the ugly beast charged me!"

"He made a lot of noise getting away from you," I said ironically.

The sun had come out after a struggling attempt, and

REREMAI. THIS IS THE BRUTE THAT CAME TO LIFE AND TOOK POSSESSION OF THE COCKPIT

PLATE LXXXVI

SEVEN HUNDRED AND TWO POUNDS! VERY HARD ON TACKLE

PLATE LXXXVII

the rest of the day promised to be fair. We took the dingy and rowed to the mouth of the river, and cast our flies along the base of the cliff where the river water could be seen clearly defined in the green of the lake water. It was a singular fact, because both waters were wonderfully clear.

The ribbed sand, so beautifully and symmetrically lined; the tremendous cliff, all green with moss and lichen; the transparent water, sparkling, luminous; and lastly the red-sided trout swimming in and out of the shadows—all these made up for my failure to get a strike.

The Captain, eventually, had a strike from a fish neither of us saw rise; but we saw it pull, and we heard the reel shriek, and then had splendid sight of a big rainbow in the air. Four more times he leaped, the last time high above the water; after which he settled down to a fight which satisfied both Captain Mitchell and me as to the game qualities of this Oregon breed of rainbow transplanted to New Zealand waters. Upon near view we saw this trout to be short, thick and heavy, with a broad red bar from gill to tail. He was much more brilliantly and richly colored than the rainbows caught in Oregon.

This one weighed eight pounds, and was the extent of our luck that day.

When our launch returned from Taupo about sunset, it carried news of an unfortunate accident that had happened to the boatman who had helped bring our outfit from Taupo the day before. On the way back he had closed the engine room to keep out water, as the lake was still rough. Gases formed and an explosion occurred, blowing up the forward part of the launch and setting fire to the rest. He had to take to the water, and he removed part of his clothing while swimming. The night was dark and the water icy cold. When about exhausted he was thrown by the waves upon a rocky shore and managed to crawl out. As soon as he recovered sufficient strength he started on foot for Taupo, over the roughest and hardest kind of going. He bound his feet with strips of his waistcoat. At length he reached a farmhouse, where he dropped, almost dead from exposure and exhaustion.

Thus I was reminded of my remarks to the skipper of our launch on the day before, and had more proof of the necessity for two boats to travel together.

During the afternoon, when the breeze lulled, I had heard a low roar, which I took to come from falling water. Across Western Bay from our camp a beautiful white waterfall tumbled from a high cleft in the cliff, down into the lake. Naturally I thought the sound had been made by this fall; but when I went to bed and lay quietly I heard the sound more distinctly. It struck me as a strange low rolling roar, not now at all like that of falling water. It came intermittently several times before I went to sleep.

During the night I awoke. My watch told the hour of midnight. At first there appeared to be a profound silence; but presently I heard the ripple of the river over the bar, and the wash of the lake. Next I heard an owl hoot; two sharp weird notes repeated at intervals. After that rose the strange low distant roar. Was it falling water? I lay there between a thrill and a tremble. The first part of that sound might have been a waterfall, but the latter was not. Muttering, rumbling, subterranean roar! I imagined I felt the ground quiver. Voice of the volcano! There was no doubt about it; and the realization was one of great import to me. To read of the quaking of the earth, and to have some one tell of the growl of cataclysmic portent of an eruption were enough to stir excitement and dread; but to feel that the solid ground was as unstable as water and to have my ears filled with the terrible rumble were things vastly more agitating. In the silence and blackness of the night the volcano roar seemed unearthly. Indeed it came from under the earth, like storm wind rushing through a vast empty hall! I heard it at intervals for what seemed hours and it worked upon my imagination and emotion as no other single phenomenon of nature ever had.

Next day was cloudy and raw. Captain Mitchell and Baker took the launch and went for a day's fishing on the Waihaha River. I chopped wood, worked around camp, listened to the birds and the murmuring river, wrote up my notes, and cast a fly endlessly and vainly over the dark waters at the mouth of the river. I could see rainbow trout, but they could likewise see me. At the end of a long day, somehow full of contentment for me, the two anglers returned from the Waihaha to report their luck. Captain Mitchell caught two fish, one three, and the other six pounds and a half. Baker drew a blank. They did not go far up the river into swift water. Maoris who lived at the mouth reported a splendid waterfall two miles up the canyon, which we decided to visit.

After supper I tried night fishing with the Captain, using the large homemade flies Ricket had brought us. The cliff was one sheer wall of ebony that towered seemingly to the heavens. Stars were innumerable and bright in a dark blue sky. Above the left wall I saw Orion sloping as always toward the west. Then almost over my head burned the Southern Cross, with its great stars white and blazing. What a singular sensation the spectacle gave me, aside from its splendor! Fishing under the Southern Cross! It was almost unbelievable. I would make a cast into the mysterious darkness between our boat and the cliff, then while gently moving my fly by a twitch of my rod I would gaze up at the Southern Cross. Suddenly I had a fierce strike that nearly jerked

my rod out of my hand and certainly made the line shriek
off the reel; but my star-gazing had left me unprepared.
The trout leaped with a sounding souse. Then my line
went slack. After that I tried to fish with more care, and
succeeded for a while, until the plaguy old volcano
began to rumble. Again I was distracted. So I wound
in my line, sat down, and gave myself up in peace to the
profundity of the heavens and the mystery of the firma-
ment. I quite forgot that I had a comrade in the boat,
an ardent angler who while casting a fly could not have
seen the Halley comet or heard Mt. Pelee erupt. He
made his presence known to me, however, by hitting me
with his back cast. Whereupon I moved to the stern
seat.

Later I absently felt around for my leader and my
fly, and finding what I thought must be they, I proceeded to try to fasten the hook of the fly in the tiny ring
on the rod, placed there for that purpose. It was so dark
I could not stick the hook through the little ring.

Suddenly the feathery-covered hook went snip! and
whipped out of my fingers. At the same instant I heard
a swish.

"Cap," I said thoughtfully, "did you just make a
cast?"

"Yes; but there was something funny about it," he
replied.

"Ahuh! It sure was funny," I returned grimly. "I
had your fly in my fingers and was trying to fasten the
hook on my rod when you made that cast."

"By gad! You don't say so! Might have hooked you.
This night fishing is not so much to my liking."

"R. C. would say it's the bunk. Let's go back to
camp."

During the next several days we learned many things.
Captain Mitchell caught nine trout, the largest eight

pounds; Baker caught three, and I half a dozen. A few
of these fish were in poor condition; "slabs" the boatmen
called them. As a matter of fact, they were starved fish.
Flat as a thin slab, pale silver color underneath, pale
green on the back, and deformed toward the tail, they
were indeed miserable-looking trout.

In connection with this it may be well to repeat that
the Taupo trout were originally rainbow stock from
Oregon. They grew and multiplied so remarkably in the
lake waters and rivers that it was beyond all precedent.
I was told that the record rainbow weighed thirty-eight
pounds, and the record brown trout, also stocked from
abroad, weighed forty pounds. Twenty-five-pound fish
were common, and fourteen-pound ones were the average
weight. In the swift rivers these fish gave a wonderful
fight, and were taken on salmon tackle. In the lake the
fish were equally as game, but of course did not make
such a fight in the still water. The Tongariro River was
heralded as the greatest trout stream in all the world;
and other rivers were not far behind.

The trout became so abundant that feed grew scarce,
and the government had the lakes seined, resulting in the
catching of tons of rainbow. That appeared to help the
situation. But the same condition returned, and at the
time of our visit it was plain there were too many trout
and too little feed. Some of ours, however, notably the
females, were plump and rosy, deep-bodied and graceful,
and enduringly strong.

We found our Rogue River flies too small, and that
the very largest of salmon flies were not too large. The
local fishermen use very dark flies, almost black, with
long feathery streamers, a little red or buff. We got to
making our own flies; clumsy enough things they were,
but effective. The several large salmon flies, of course,
we lost. There is a huge rainbow trout out there yet

swimming around with my salmon fly in his jaw. I hope he gets rid of it.

These rainbow seldom rose to the surface to take a fly; they waited till it sank. I saw a good many dart at my fly, only to refuse it because in my position I could not give the fly more movement. They took a slow fly, but not too slow, and the cast was the better if allowed to go deep. I had several heavy trout strike with a tremendous rush, hook themselves and leap to tear free.

Captain Mitchell's usual method of casting and slowly working his fly, with little jerks of the rod, did not need any change. It was ideal; but my method, learned over swift water, where after the cast a bag of line is drawn down by the current, carrying the fly faster, was not suitable for the quiet lake. I had to try to learn over, a task not to be conquered on one fishing trip. Fishing is all difficulty, something evermore to overcome. That is why it is my favorite recreation, work or pleasure.

Following those several days of exploration and adjustment to the strange water and conditions, we started for an all-day trip to the Waihaha River.

We traveled along the precipitous cliffs and close to the waterfall that had become a part of our surroundings, both in its slender whiteness falling over the gray wall and in its often-heard roar. Beyond that round bold promontory, we came to a great break in the cliffs, through which the Waihaha flowed in two streams into the lake. At the mouth of this little river, Ricket and two other fishermen, a few weeks before our arrival, caught in one night sixty-two trout weighing six hundred and eighty pounds, the largest twenty pounds; all in the dark and on the fly! It was amazing to me. He explained that the trout came in out of the deep water at night and collected at the mouth of the river. They could be taken by wading or by casting from a boat.

Ever since my interest had been roused in New Zealand waters, I had been reading of incredible bags of fish, taken by this angler, or by that group of anglers. Seldom were these records below a hundredweight, and often they went to tons. I could not understand how one fisherman could catch a ton of rainbow trout in a month, fishing only the best of the days. After I learned about the heavy tackles and the spinners, and especially the night fishing with flies, I was a great deal better informed.

The morning we selected to devote to the Waihaha River was dull and gray, with a cold breeze across the lake. We went ashore on the sandy beach that stretched from wall to wall of the canyon of the Waihaha; and laden with tackle, lunch, cameras, waders, etc., we started across the flat cut-over bottomland through which the river wound. The Maori huts stood back among clumps of trees, some of which were pines. We saw natives working in potato fields and milking cows. Those we approached were friendly and agreeable, no doubt glad to get the half crown a head they charged for our fishing. Half a mile up the valley the river ran deep, dark and broad, perhaps sixty yards in width, and looked very inviting to a fisherman. The banks, however, were ugly with multitudes of stumps of the *ti* trees that had been cleared off, and piles of brush, and cattle trails and corrals.

Beyond the farms we found a trail leading up the narrowing valley, through heavy fern growth and an occasional thicket. All the information we had obtained was that the falls were two miles up the river. The trail then was an agreeable surprise. It led over level ground for a while, then began to climb over ridges that sloped down from the bluffs. We got high enough to look down upon the winding river and to see what wonderful fishing water it would be if the banks were cleared. It ran shallow, swift and deep by turns. Some of the dark swirling green holes in the bends of the stream were so beautiful and promising that it was almost impossible to pass by them. A jungle of green trees, ferns, brush and vines, with the pampas-like grass in open places, grew denser as we advanced.

I was the first to hear the roar of falling water, and heralded the event with a shout. That spurred us on, and soon we turned a bend in the canyon to be greeted by a most wonderful scene. We were hundreds of feet up the side of the canyon. Ahead of us the great gray walls closed in to a cleft, out of which shot a white fan-shaped waterfall, to tumble down into a very large dark-green pool. A wide crescent-shaped beach of sand stretched round fully one-half of this little lake. On the right side, under the green-foliaged cliff, the outlet of the pool slid narrow and deep.

We were on the wrong side of the river, and had to turn back. Presently from a high bank I espied a wide shallow place with gravel bottom, and I was sure we could get down there and cross. Captain Mitchell was doubtful, and Baker offered to bet me we could not. I took him up. Captain Mitchell went far below and found a way down to the river, and coming back to a point beneath us, where I designated, he waded across easily. Thus I won my wager with Baker. To get down here appeared likewise impossible to the Englishman. It was an almost perpendicular slant of sand. But I ran down, zigzag, on seven-league boots, landing breathless but safe. Whereupon Baker and Morton followed more leisurely. The Captain and I had to pack them both across, not an easy task; but it was necessary, as they did not have waders. Then we crashed, tore and worked a passage through the jungle to the wide sandy beach.

THE MAKO SHARK, NEW ZEALAND'S GAMEST FISH (Plates lxxxviii to xci)

s to 20 feet in length and a ton in weight. The most terrific of leapers, endangering the lives of anglers. The last picture shows Captain Mitchell's 1200-pound mako in the air just before breaking off.)

PLATE LXXXVIII

PLATE LXXXIX

PLATE XC

PLATE XCI

There the view was even more striking, as we looked up at the falls, the towering cliffs and the narrow cleft. The sandy beach was something to see and walk upon. Not a footprint! The piercing notes of tuis and bell-birds sounded above the roar of the waterfall.

We waded into the wonderful pool, over clear white sand, Baker on the left by the rocks, Captain Mitchell in the center where the swift current bore down, and I on the right next to the mighty lichened and mossed cliff, under which ran a deep dark channel. Here I would cast until the icy water drove me back to the fire. Altogether we put in about two hours there, during which I had one strike, which I missed, Baker had no luck, and Captain Mitchell caught four rainbows, one of them weighing eleven pounds. None of these fish leaped, or broke water. The eleven-pounder made a hard fight, running up under the falls and the ledge on my side, but eventually was worn out and beached, a magnificent male trout, very dark bronze and red, with scarcely decipherable spots. His jaws were like those of a wolf.

Somewhat disgusted and disappointed with my luck, I started back ahead of the others, intending to fish the stream down. Certainly I took a great deal upon myself, for only in a few places could the water be fished. I saw a great many big rainbows, and several brown trout of large dimensions, most of which saw me before I saw them. At last I came to a grand pool in a bend, a dark green whirling hole, full of rocks and snags, overgrown by brush and trees. To cap the climax, on a sloping beach of sand, across the pool, I espied a brown trout of at least twenty pounds. Whereupon I began to try to cast a fly over him. It was not a long distance, scarcely seventy feet; but owing to brush behind me I failed every time to make any cast at all. Still I persisted. After each try, when I caught my fly in the brush, I would plod back and extricate it, then break down that particular offending bush. A dozen or more times I did this. No good! I could not reach him. Naturally I grew resolved to cast a fly over that wonderful fish or die in the attempt. To this end I edged farther out on the bank, and finally secured a most precarious footing on a thick mat of bush. I shuddered at the depth of dark water under me, and what might happen if I slipped in. Standing here I essayed more casts, and got out more line every time; but each time when I made the cast that would have covered the trout I fouled the brush above and back of me. So I went to work and broke all the brush down. Upon returning to my task I surely felt that something was going to happen, thrilling and eventful. So I whipped out my line, farther and farther. Meanwhile the rest of the party had arrived and stood above me on the trail, most noisy and interested onlookers. As good luck would have it, on my third cast I got the line out beautifully and the big fly dropped beyond and above the brown trout. It sank and floated down, while my heart stopped and my gaze strained on that fish. He showed clearly in three feet of water. He was very dark, broad, and speckled. When the fly floated, with the little jerks I gave it, right over him, very close, he twitched his tail, and let the feathery lure float by.

After all my work and zeal and hope! He would not rise. I let my fly float on, forgot about it, and vainly watched that beautiful fish. Suddenly I heard a tremendous splash below me, downstream behind the overhanging foliage, and the next second I felt a vicious tug at my line. My rod nearly flew out of my hand, and my reel screeched. Then out from the middle of the green pool like an arrow shot a trout red-barred and silvery; and out he leaped, tumbling high, glistening in the sunlight. My audience yelled vociferous encouragement,

while I bounded back to the bank, and ran around upstream, winding my reel madly. What luck that the
trout ran upstream! By the time I got even with his
position he turned back, but I shut down on my reel, and
we had it out right there. It was break him off or hold
him. If he got a run downstream my case was hopeless.
So I held him as tightly as I dared. Once I thought he
was gone, for he pulled the line away from me. Yet instead of going on he leaped high. If he had kept up that
run he would have escaped. From that time I held him
to the middle of the pool; and in what seemed an endless
fight to me I bested him, and slipped him out on the sand,
a live rainbow if there ever was one, and something too
beautiful to describe.

My comrades took to the trail and went on, meaning to
try the mouth of the river. I, however, hung back and
tried to find places where I could fish. These were few
and far between. Late in the afternoon I came to the
largest pool in the Waihaha, with open banks on each
side. A sand bar sloped in from my side. Across was
shelving bank and deep black water. I waded in and
essayed a long cast. It took three attempts to put the fly
where I desired, but at last it alighted exactly where I
imagined a trout might lie. My fly sank out of my sight.
Then there came a bulge on the water, a swirl that could
have been made only by a churning fish tail. I recognized that. My nerves tingled. Something leaped in
me. Then instinctively I struck, and came up hard on a
heavy fish. He gave me a tremendous pull. My rod
bent over straight, and my line, despite my holding tight,
slipped through my hand. I waded out and back up the
bank, dragging the heavy fish away from the danger zone
across from me. Every instant I expected a leap, but
none came. Suddenly he changed his tugging tactics
and darted up the pool, taking twenty yards of line.

Next he wheeled and sped back, swift as a flash, and turned the curve out of the deep hole into a wide shallow place, where there was only clean white sand. I ran along the bank, winding in my line, and presently I saw him, dark red and black, and then silver, whirling over and over in the water just like a steelhead. These were bad maneuvers for me and I certainly expected disaster. Such action always tears out the hook if kept up long enough. Luckily he gave that up and went to making short runs for the opposite bank. These I checked by holding harder than I ever did before on any small fish. What amazed me was the endurance of this rainbow. He kept that sort of tactics up until my left arm was numb and my right hand good and tired. All of this fight I saw perfectly in the crystal water. He did not make a single jump; but he gave me the greatest battle I ever had with a trout in still water. At last when he lay out on the moss I had an almost irresistible desire to return him to the river. He was long, broad, thick, with very wide tail. His color was very dark bronze and silver, with only a tinge of rose through which the black dots showed. I estimated him at nine pounds, but later I found he did not weigh so much. I had about all I wanted to carry down to the point. These two river fish added greatly to my anticipation of the Tongariro.

CHAPTER XIII

DURING our stay at the Waihoro River I spent some enjoyable hours trying to see some of the song birds that sang so sweetly.

Hard work and patience always bring reward, whether the task be fishing, studying birds, or any occupation. Behind camp along the great cliff wall stood a dense forest, mostly *ti* trees, among which at any time from sunrise to dark the wild birds made melody.

A couple of kingfishers made our camp a rendezvous, and flitted to and fro above the shallow river, or sat on a dead willow branch, watching for some little fish to dive at. Of all the kingfishers I ever observed, this species was the most singular. He was small and appeared all head. That was black and armed with a most formidable bill, thick, long and heavy. The huge size of his head made the bird seem grotesque. He had a small plump body, gray breast and blue back, and a short black tail, very slender, that he bobbed up and down all the time he sat perched upon a branch. This bird did not utter any sound during the numerous occasions I watched him. When he flew he shone resplendent in the sun.

The trees were full of the little yellow blighties, named from their very good habit of eating the insect blight. They were about the size of canaries, a light soft green in color, with breast dull gray. The eyes appeared to have circles or bars of light around them. A sweet twittering filled the woods wherever these little birds were.

I liked especially the fantails. What delicate lovely birds! They too were small in size, with graceful tiny head, dark in color, and bill so diminutive as to be almost impossible to see. The tail was the distinguishing feature of these birds. It was long and light-colored, and when spread made a perfect fan, the two center feathers of which were dark. I often watched the fantails. On one occasion two gave me a pretty exhibition of their feeding. It was early in the morning and I was back in the woods just at the edge of an open place. I stood motionless. These birds flew down and perched on a snag above me. Then one darted out, fluttered and whirled, and returned to his perch. The other made nearly the same maneuver. I saw the insects in the air. A fantail would flutter out a few feet—snip!—then back to his perch. Finally I saw one actually catch an insect; but if I watched the birds I could not detect their prey. It was only by looking up at the sky and locating a tiny gnat or moth that I could see the actual tragedy. Snip! What vicious little bills, considering their size! The noise was as hard to hear as the bills were to see.

I was about to make my presence known when both took after the same insect, quite a large fluttering creature. The birds practically were in midair in collision. That seemed to anger them and one flew after the other, uttering fierce little notes. They darted within a foot of my face, and all around over my head; and finally the pursuit took them off into the woods.

The tui and bell-bird were the particular objects of my spare moments spent under the trees. I saw many of the tuis, and one very close at hand. It was a bird of dull color, almost drab in the light that I had. But I distinguished the white surplice-like tufts, just below the neck, that give this bird the name parson bird. He appeared smaller than a robin, larger than a lark. He was a wonderful songster. I had the luck to see this tui while he uttered five different notes. First the series of deep lonely notes, very similar to that of our hermit thrush. This song is one of the sweetest and loveliest of all bird melodies. Next was a single pealing note, wild and plaintive, that had no counterpart in any bird sounds I had ever heard. After that note, which he uttered at intervals for a while, he was silent, and flitted to another tree. I followed and again got close. Then he gave out two whistles, short and sweet. He succeeded that with an exact imitation of a spitting cat. At first I was sure I had been deceived; but I heard him make that sound at least a dozen times. Moreover, I saw him do it. This was an amazing sound to come from such a sweet-throated bird. Again he flitted out of my sight. I did not want to make any sound, and as the brush was thick I had to crane my neck to try to catch sight of this tui again, but I could not. Suddenly from right where he had gone came a marvelous bell note. I listened, tingling with expectancy. It was not repeated. I could not be sure that this note was the imitation of the bell-bird. It might have come from a real bell-bird, for there were several in the little forest. I had to be content with having heard that perfect note at close range. It was the purest, the sweetest, the wildest and most melancholy, the most melodious that I had ever listened to. It enhanced the glamour that seemed to hang around my impressions of the bell-bird.

For six whole days we never saw the peaks of the volcano and the snow-capped mountains. Always lost in clouds, at sunrise a rosy tinged canopy, at noonday the massed cumulous pageants that hung motionless for hours, and at sunset broken gold and white reefs that showed the steep black slopes of the mountains behind. For days the roar of the volcano had been intermittent and only a low rumble. Often when the wind blew from the west I mistook the roar of the waterfall for the disturbing subterranean disturbance.

There was fog, too, in the early mornings; a mountain mist that drifted down the canyon and out over the lake, breaking up in the rays of the sun. Lower and lower, inch by inch, the Waihoro River went down, until in front of our camp it flowed scarcely a foot deep. Ruben, one of our camp boys, shot a wild pig, after which we were not bothered by the rootings and sniffings and squealings around our tents.

During these ideal days we fished as always, earnestly and indefatigably, Baker and Mitchell practically all the time, while I put in mornings and evenings, and another full day up the Waihaha. Compared with trout fishing in the United States our luck was phenomenal. Captain Mitchell increased his score to twenty-eight; Baker his to thirteen, and I ran mine to twenty-three. All our fish were large, not for Taupo waters, but in relation to the size we were accustomed to take. Eight and nine pounders were not uncommon. Both Baker and Mitchell got eleven-pound fish. Some of these took the fly voraciously and on light tackle gave an angler all he wanted for the time being.

I took two seven-pounders and one eight-pounder at the mouth of the Waihoro, where the river water ran rippling along the cliff. Here under the overhanging ledges

WITH THE MAORIS AT ROTORUA (Plates xcii to xcv)
(Note the Maori custom of rubbing noses in salutation.)

PLATE XCII

PLATE XCIII

PLATE XCIV

PLATE XCV

of amber moss and the leaning green foliage the big rainbows lurked, waiting for insects and flies to drop from above. I hooked one of these fish without knowing he was there, but the other two had risen for flies, splashing on the surface, leaving the telltale widening circles into which I cast. The rise, the seeing of the trout, the strike, and the subsequent battle were matters dear to heart and memory.

My nine-pound rainbow, however, I raised in a place that fascinated me profoundly aside from its satisfaction as a fishing hole. How often fishing leads a man to find beauty otherwise never seen! I am rich in having a treasure store of such places.

Around the corner from the mouth of the Waihoro there rose a cliff the like of which I never saw. It was a perpendicular fluted palisade rising to the dignity and boldness of a mountain. Seen from a distance it looked to be a gray-lined, cracked and stained wall of rock, bare near the water line, and above covered with green growths. As such it had a noble austere front, compelling the gaze; but it was near at hand that this cliff became surpassingly beautiful.

The first time I rowed under its shadow I raised and hooked my nine-pound rainbow which leaped prodigiously, limned his graceful red-and-silver bulk against the amber moss, and made such a display and such a fight that I should have always remembered the place if it had no other call to memory. But this particular cliff wall struck me as magnificent, and peculiarly haunting in its loveliness. I returned to it again and again, and visited it, in all, over a dozen times, despite the fact that I never raised another trout there.

I did not need to, I did not want to, and forgot the rod I held in my hands. At every hour of the day this crater wall was different. In the morning shade, however, when the water was still, so the reflection of stone, moss, flowers, trees, sky and cloud could be seen with the most marvelous clearness, it was at its best and transcendently lovely.

There is no way to describe a thing in nature that baffles description. Yet something can be written in the way of detail, or record. I called it a cliff wall, which indeed it was, yet that term seemed very misleading. There were walls, columns, pillars, knife-edged corners; deep fissures running back into the body of the stones, wonderful blank spaces like those of ancient Egyptian monuments; niches and ledges, crevices and hundreds of little places where seeds had blown, to grow into plant or vine or bush, holding tenaciously to the rock. At the base of the wall a dark matted amber moss grew thickly, through which the gentle movement of water made a low seeping sound.

The knife-edged corners were bare rock, dark gray or yellow, rusted or stained; and some of these extended upward a hundred feet or more, before blunting into the buttress of the overhanging brow, where the foliage grew thick and black. The reflection of these corners was beautiful in the extreme. How strange to gaze down into the clear water, seeing the stone change from gray to amber, from amber to pale green, from green to blue and violet, and then into dim obscurity! They led into the abysmal depths of this crater, which the guide reported to be thirteen hundred feet deep, straight down from the shore line. Indeed it looked to have such a depth along my cliff wall! There seemed to be a drawing fascination to gaze and gaze down as the boat slowly moved along. Every reflection differed, as did every yard of the cliff. Below hid cold stark death in a region of supreme mystery and loveliness. The shadows of trees and clouds and sky seemed to lie behind the marvelous reflections of the wall, seen through some crystal magnifying medium.

Then, loveliest of all were the minute details which made up the whole; the patches of gray fuzzy moss like the color of desert sage; and lower down velvety pads of amber moss that merged into the web of a still darker moss at the water line. Patterns of lichen delicately etched spread over the stone face, gray and green, yellow and bronze, and lastly a deep rich gold that burned in the sunlight. From the lichens and moss tiny flowers blossomed, lifting pale sweet faces to the sky, the wild white violet being conspicuous, and daisies smaller still, and a red flower so minute as to be hard to see. On ledges stood up white pink-centered flowers like mountain-laurel, and higher up sprigs of willow leaned out with creamy fuzzy blossoms. Most exquisite were the rare little forget-me-nots of New Zealand. I pulled one of the delicate stems with its marvelous tiny blue flower, five-petaled, with center circle of white and gold. This sprig had three buds, two closed and green, and a third bursting into pink. Growing wild there, this true forget-me-not was something too lovely ever to be forgotten.

All these things were near at gaze and easy to see, if so impossible to describe; but higher up there were baffling plants, vines, ferns, moss and bush, with color blending like a mosaic inlaid into the cliff wall. I could only take possession of them by sight, realizing I could never know them at close range and by name. Flowered cranny and blossoming niche, fringed ledge where graceful ferns leaned over, slant of cliff where a larger growth of moss spread like puff-balls—these led up to the bulge of wall and the *ti* trees and *kowhai*, all green now, but at Christmas time brilliant with red blossoms. Above these were the spear-leaved lancewood, and higher still the locust-like tree of palest green in all that richness of verdure. Lastly here were to be heard the bell-birds and tuis, at any time of the day, sweetly and wildly pouring out the golden treasure of their throats, to the loneliness and solitude.

CHAPTER XIV

GREATLY to our satisfaction, we had a calm day
for breaking camp on the Waihoro, and our run
around the lake to Tokaanu.   Once past the huge
buttress of the western headland, we had full view of the
beautiful Tongariro Mountain and beyond it the higher
cone, Ngauruhoe, which shot aloft puffs of creamy
smoke that mushroomed and hung in the sky.

As we neared the deep cut-in of the lake, where the
red-roofed white houses of Tokaanu stood out clearly
against the green, the high peaks dropped down behind
Pihanga Mountain.

We passed the delta of the great Tongariro River.
The three mouths of the famous river had interested me
for years.   To one so given to imagination as I, the
mouths of this river were disappointing.   They ran over
shallow sand bars into the lake.   Captain Mitchell and I
stood up on the deck of our launch the better to see.   We
ran quite close, expecting to have a good view of some
anglers fly casting in the ripples; but all we saw were
half a dozen skiffs, anchored at the several mouths of the

river, and in each an angler sitting with exceptionally long and heavy rod, and pulling his line in hand over hand. We had to wait a good time before one of them made a cast; but it was not a cast, just a fling of the line out, to let it float away with the current.

"By gad!" muttered Captain Mitchell. "That's the way they do it."

"Captain, it is not fly fishing," I said. "Most illuminating in regard to the heavy catches reported."

That alone decided us against camping at or near the delta. We had our outfit hauled up the river in a truck, and we went in cars to find a beautiful spot on a high bank, in a grove of trees, above the roaring rushing white and green Tongariro.

At last Captain Mitchell and I looked down into this trout stream, so celebrated among English anglers, and of which so much had been read by anglers of America. I could learn no word of any American ever having visited these waters.

"Shades of the Rogue River!" ejaculated the Captain.

"No, Cap, it's the green-white rushing Athabasca, which I wrote about in my story, *The Great Slave*," I replied.

Just to look at the Tongariro made us both happy. We could see bend after bend, pool after pool, rapid after rapid, all from the high bank at camp. There was a roaring rapid just above, not one of the deep-toned thundering falls peculiar to the Rogue, but a long narrow channel of white water, green at the edges, and just noisy enough not to be fearful. You did not think, "Suppose I should fall in there!" You just listened to the low murmuring roar. The Rogue, most wonderful of American trout streams, is a deep swift cold canyon-walled and rock-rapided river, hurrying down to the sea, with but few shallows and bars. The Tongariro appeared to have about the same volume of water, pale blue-green in color, exquisitely clear, too clear for fishing, and though a swift river, still it was not wild in its hurry to escape the confines of its banks. It was what I call a gravel river, there being bars and banks, all heavy gravel, and a river-bed of the same. In some places high banks of sand stood out of the green foliage, but for the most part the shores were sloping and covered with dense bush. Perhaps the most striking feature about the Tongariro in this section, six to ten miles above the delta, was the number and character of the islands. They were really gravel bars, under water when the river was in flood, and at low water picturesque green and gray islands around which the channels and rifts ran. Just below our camp the swift river broadened and slowed, with a wide sand and gravel beach on our side and a high bluff on the other, against which the current banked. From these points it separated into three channels, running in different directions, and dropped considerably to a lower level of the river. The channel that curved westward under our bank was narrow, shallow and boisterous. The middle channel took most of the river volume, and it roared down, deep and fast. The other channel ran glancing and smooth away to the southward, and dropped out of sight.

Our camp was situated in a grove of *ti* and *kowhai* trees. Behind the grove spread an oval green flat, dominated by two huge pine trees. Three poplar trees, also familiar reminders of my native land, stood up straight and tall, dressed in the gold of autumn, which contrasted beautifully with the surrounding bright greens. Far on the horizon rose the magnificent mountain range, wreathed at dawn by sun-flushed clouds, clear and sharp and dark at noonday, and at sunset half obscured in lilac haze.

[179]

It always takes time on new waters to find the best places and the right way to fish. Our Maori guide, Hoka Down, who owned the land round about, said the river was at the worst possible stage for fishing. A good hard rain was needed to start the trout running up from the lake. Still, he believed we might pick up a trout here and there, occasionally. I liked Hoka. He was jolly and fat, and he always wore a pleasant smile. He appeared well educated and sincere. He confided to Captain Mitchell his concern and regret regarding my visit to the Tongariro at a time when I would not get any of the wonderful fishing for which this river is noted all over the world.

The other side of the river looked by far the best, but we could not get across. We spent our first day crashing through the matted jungle of ferns and wading over the channels of the islands above. The water was so cold that it absolutely paralyzed me through my waders. We built fires as we went along, waded and cast, and then splashed out to get warm. We tried an endless variety of flies. Captain Mitchell was partial to English flies— the Silver Doctor, Thunder and Lightning, Jock Scott, Sandy Special, etc.—and I pinned my faith as of old to the Rogue River flies. We did not raise any fish during the morning. Mr. Wiffin argued that in New Zealand sunshine was best for fishing. It had certainly been cloudy and dark, the very best kind of weather for trout fishing in the United States. Then about noon the sun did shine.

I put on one of the long light flies made from the checkered feathers of the bittern, and which had somewhat the motion of a little minnow in the water. I had used this with some success at the mouth of the Waihoro.

Casting this far out over the tail of a pool, where the water began to slide toward the rapid below, I let it

The Rainbow Trout in Fairy Spring (Plates xcvi to xcvii)
(*These fish run up to 12 pounds and are free to come and go at will. They will eat out of the hand.*)

Plate XCVI

Plate xcvii

swing round, and as it straightened out I had a good solid strike. Always that sensation will be electrifying. It elicited a shout from me.

"Hey, Cap! I'm fast to my first Tongariro rainbow!"

The trout did not show or leap, but he pulled hard enough to make me overestimate his weight. That proved to be six pounds. The rainbow trout never had his name more perfectly illustrated than in this colorful specimen.

We were encouraged to fish out the afternoon, working downstream and conquering obstacles in the way of dense thickets and slippery rocks. Late in the day I found myself at the pool just above the rapids which marked our camp. I chose the lower end, as seems always my way, and waded out to cast far across under the willows. I felt there must be a trout in the dark swirling water. So I cast and cast, all in vain; then, just to try to imitate Captain Mitchell in his everlasting patience and persistence, I kept on casting. The time came when I got a strike; a nibbling little tug! He had missed the hook. Whereupon I went on emulating Captain Mitchell. Soon I had another tug. This time I struck smartly. He was too quick. By now I had an audience in the shape of Morton, and Breckon, the expert photographer from the *Auckland Weekly*, both of whom had cameras ready. Thus encouragement was balanced against my exasperation, and I returned to my casting with more vim than ever. Then I had another touch. My line whipped up lightly, causing me to conclude the trout was a little fellow. Nevertheless I wanted more than ever to outwit him; and I cast with utmost care and precision, and with strung faculties. After perhaps as many as a dozen casts over the same place the trout rose for the fourth time, and I hooked him. To my amaze he felt solid, heavy, active. In one wrestling whirl he rid himself of the hook.

"By gosh!" I soliloquized. "Too slick for me! . . . And to think he fooled me into believing he was little."

Next morning we fished up a small stream that emptied into the Tongariro near camp. It appeared to be full of small trout, running up to three pounds. They rose to the fly, struck hard, and fought valiantly in the swift water. Several miles up this stream we came to a beautiful valley where the water ran level and quiet between banks of most luxuriant beauty. They were lined with the exquisite silver plumes, resembling pampas grass and known as *toi-toi*, and masses of bright green mint and watercress, yellow flowers, and clumps of low *ti* trees.

It was next to impossible to cast a fly over these verdant banks into the water. Yet we managed it occasionally; and when we got any kind of fly floating down the clear dark deep water near the watercress, there would be a swirl and a vicious tug. These rainbows were dark-backed and rosy-sided, some of them even gold in color. We lost many, and some we let go. Captain Mitchell lost six trout straight and the fact tickled me so that I conceived a vain notion that I would beat him this day, anyway. Nevertheless, though I started five ahead of him and kept going strong, in the end he forged ahead of me, catching twenty to my thirteen. Baker got five. There were many funny incidents, paramount of which was Captain Mitchell chasing some half-wild pigs. He had just landed a fine trout and laid it on the moss, when two pigs appeared. As he advised Baker to look out for one which went for his trout, the other pig seized Captain Mitchell's trout and ran off with it flopping from his mouth. The Captain gave chase. I heard the other fellows yelling, and turned in time to see Captain Mitchell running with all his might, and kicking the pig at every two jumps. His last kick hurt him vastly more than it did the pig, spraining a toe that had been injured during the war. The pig got away with the Captain's largest trout. The language our usually mild comrade indulged in was profoundly equal to any ever voiced by an angler.

We trudged home through brush almost as colorful and fragrant as my own purple sage, with a beautiful sunset in our faces, the mountains rising clear and grand on each side, and the melodious roar of Tongariro filling our ears.

"By Jove! What a perfect day!" exclaimed Alma Baker.

We learned from a driver who brought us supplies from Tokaanu that there were fifty rods between what he called the Bridge and the Delta camps. Fifty rods meant, of course, fifty anglers. They were not making any catches, as the trout had not begun to run up the river. At the three mouths, however, fishermen were making big bags, so the Auckland papers reported. One man, in two days, caught over two hundred pounds of rainbow trout, averaging eleven pounds. His largest was fifteen pounds, which put up a great fight, so the report read. This angler spent as much as from ten to twenty minutes landing a fish, etc., etc., etc.

All this made good reading, and it was such stuff that had puzzled me when it came before my eyes back in the States. In fact it was simply incredible. In the light of my experience and observation, and with personal contact with New Zealanders like Baker, Wiffin and Breckon, all with my party, I finally arrived at the truth about such tactics. I do not mean that the reports in the papers were untrue or exaggerated. I simply found out that they misrepresented the fishing. All on the fly! So the papers invariably stated. But it was not fly fishing, casting with light five or six ounce rods, with light lines and leaders, such as anglers know in my country. These anglers, almost without exception, used fourteen-foot salmon rods; rods that I could land a swordfish on! In fact my hickory rod that landed nine broadbills and the seven-hundred-and-four-pound black Marlin was no heavier. The lures used were very large salmon flies, or still heavier homemade ones, with line and leaders to match; or else, surely mostly, they used spinners or artificial minnows, armed with triple hooks. Captain Mitchell and I found a number of spoons and spinners sticking in the brush and on mossy rocks along the shore of the Tongariro.

This explains the unbelievable catch of two hundred pounds of rainbow trout averaging eleven pounds, by one man in two days. It would take Captain Mitchell or me a long time to land one eleven pound trout in the Tongariro; and indeed we were to learn just how long it took and how hard it was to do.

Mr. Wiffin, who had charge of my visit to Taupo and the Tongariro, was an agent for the New Zealand government. He was a dry-fly fisherman, which of course meant an expert with the lightest of tackle. He introduced fly fishing in New Zealand waters, and had converted a few other Wellington anglers to the wonderful sport of rainbow-trout fishing on delicate tackle. He said to me in part:

"I never fish the Tongariro, because I don't approve of the methods of the crowd of anglers who fish this grand river. Their methods and tackle are as primitive as you found that of the salt-water anglers at Cape Brett. The idea appears to be to catch as many trout as possible in the quickest possible time. To get the fish! That's the slogan."

This, of course, has been the prevailing mode in all

countries during the developing stage of angling. It really comes from primitive ancestors, as far back as the cave man. "Bringing home the bacon," as the hunter says, has come down to us from forebears who had to kill meat to eat.

I have always tried in my stories, whether narrative or otherwise, to make them interesting and thrilling, and then to serve the turn of instruction, as Stevenson so aptly put it. Hence the explanation above.

I suppose many New Zealand anglers will inquire, as I am an advocate of the heaviest of specially made tackle for the great tiger fish of the sea, why I put such stress on the use of delicate and light tackle for these wonderful rainbows of the Tongariro. I suppose, at least I hope, the answer to that can be found in the perusal of my story, material for which and the writing of which cost me so much labor and pains.

Hoka, our genial Maori guide, whom I had begun to like very well indeed, averred one morning that the trout had begun to run up the river, for he saw them. Both Captain Mitchell and I could verify this. To our delight and also exasperation we saw them too; but to make these rainbows rise to an ordinary fly was something which would tax the patience of a saint, not to mention a good degree of skill. The Captain did it, and so did I, but at the expense of infinite labor. We resorted to large Rogue River flies, mostly number four, and then to salmon flies number two, and finally we got to dressing our own flies. This was fun for me. Some of the outlandish lures I dressed up should have scared a rainbow trout out of his wits. Nevertheless they answered the purpose, and one of them, a fly so extraordinary that I could not make another like it, turned out to be a "killer." The only difficulty about large flies was that they were hard to cast. By diligent practice and strenuous effort, however, I at length achieved considerable distance, making an average of sixty feet, often seventy, and rarely even eighty feet. And when I saw that gaudy fly shoot out to such extreme distance I certainly felt exultant and vain.

We had word of another record catch of eleven fish at the mouth of the Tongariro. This was given us by Mr. Gilles, the mail driver, who stopped at our camp on an errand. He saw the fish and vouched for their height; a fourteen-pound average, with largest weighing sixteen and one-half pounds. All caught on a fly at night! But no other information had been vouchsafed. I asked Mr. Gilles many questions about this remarkable catch, very few of which could he answer. He was himself a fisherman of long experience, a native of Tokaanu, and it was his opinion the trout were caught by the fisherman letting out a large fly or spinner a hundred or two hundred feet from the boat, and then drawing it back by hand until he had a strike. I shared this opinion.

By climbing to the bluff above the river, when the sun was high, he could see the big trout lying deep in the pale-green crystal water; ten, twelve and fifteen pound rainbows, and an occasional brown trout, huge and dark, upward of twenty pounds. This was a terrible, although glad experience for Captain Mitchell and me. To sight such wonderful fish and not get a rise from them! Alma Baker took it more philosophically, and considered the privilege of seeing them quite enough. Cap and I, however, wanted to feel one of those warriors at the end of a line. In the pool below camp we tried at sunrise, through the day, at sunset and then after dark. Fly fishing at night was an awful experience for me. I got snarled in the line. I continually hit my rod with my fly, and half the time it spun round the rod, entailing most patient labor. Moreover, I was standing through the chill of night in ice-cold water. Finally I whipped the big hook in the back of my coat. That gave me sufficient excuse to go back to camp. What joy the camp fire! Captain Mitchell returned presently, wet and shivering. He did not complain of the cold water, but he lamented a great deal over the loss of his best fly. He had snagged it on a rock and nearly drowned himself trying to rescue it.

Next morning while the rest of the party were at breakfast I stole down the bank and made a cast into the swirling waters. I made another, and when I strove to retrieve the line, lo! it was fast to something that moved. I struck, and I hooked a trout. For fear he might rush out into the swift current I held him harder than I would otherwise, and thus tired him out before he could take advantage of me. When I was sure of him, a fine seven-pounder rolling in the clear water, I yelled loudly. The whole breakfast contingent rushed pellmell to the bank, and to say they were amazed would be putting it mildly.

"By Jove!" ejaculated Baker. "You lucky devil! That's a fine fish."

"I wondered where you were," added Mitchell, with an experienced eye on my fish.

"You fellows have to have your tea, you know," I responded cheerfully.

That was a prelude to a strenuous day for all of us. Baker elected to fish the pools below camp, where he did not have to wade. Hoka took Captain Mitchell and me, accompanied by Morton, up the river.

"Only a little way, about a mile," said Hoka, with the smile that always robbed me of a retort. It was a long, long mile before we even got off the road; and even a short mile in heavy waders, three pairs of woolen socks, and iron-studded clumsy wading boots was always quite sufficient. I can pack a gun and walk light-footed far up and down canyons, but the wading paraphernalia burdens me down.

Hoka led us into a fern trail, one of those exasperating trails where the ferns hook your fishing line and leader and will not let go. Then he arrived at a precipitous bluff under which an unseen river roared musically. It was not the Tongariro. The Captain naturally wanted to know how we got down.

"We go right over," replied Hoka, and with the remark he disappeared. We heard crashings in the ferns. Next I went "right over." I held my rods high above my head and trusted my seven-league eight-ton boots to the depths. Then I went right over, but also down, my only concern being my rods. When at last I arrived at a comparative level, I awaited to see what would happen to my comrades. I knew there would be a fall all right. Soon I heard what might have been a rhinoceros plowing down the ferny cliff; but it was only Captain Mitchell, who arrived beside me hot, furious, forgetful of all save his precious pipe, which a tenacious fern still clung to. The real fun, however, came with Morton. Our genial cinematographer was burdened with cameras, also a pair of iron-hoofed boots that I had insisted he must wear. I have no idea how Morton got down, unless he fell all the way. We heard him talking vociferously to the obstructing ferns. At last he arrived, red of face, and grimly hanging on to his load.

"Dash it!" he panted. "You guys—must have had— persuaders to get down—that bally place."

The term guys Morton had learned from me and the word persuaders was a joke with us. While at our salt-water fishing on the coast I wrote about the teasers we trolled behind the boat, to attract swordfish. Whereupon an Englishman sent me a letter in which he said, "I note you use persuaders."

Hoka was waiting for us with his disarming smile.

"You came down easy," he said. "But this panel over the river will be hard."

"Huh! What's a panel!" I asked. "Hoka, I've begun to have suspicions about you.

He soon showed us the panel. It was no less than a rickety pole bridge, swung on wires attached to branches of trees, and spanning a dark rushing little river that must have been beautiful at some other time. Just now it seemed a treacherous one. How the current swept on, down, down, rushing, swirling, gurgling under the dark over-reaching trees!

Hoka went first. He weighed seventeen stone, which in our language is over two hundred pounds; and I felt that if the panel held him it would certainly hold me. He crossed safely and quite quickly for so large a man. I went next. Such places rouse a combative spirit in me, and that made the crossing something different. Nevertheless when I was right in the middle, where the thin crooked poles bent under my heavy boots, I gazed down into the murky water with grim assurance of what might happen if the poles broke. I got across, proving how unnecessary the stirring of my imagination often is.

Once safe on the bank I was tempted to yell something facetious to Morton and Mitchell, but I desisted, for this was hardly the place for humor. They reached our side without mishap, and then again we beat into the jungle of ferns and *ti* trees. It was hard going, but soon I heard the mellow roar of the Tongariro, and with that growing louder and louder I found less concern about difficulties. We came at length into an open thicket of *ti* brush, bisected by shallow waterways and dry sandy spaces, through which we emerged to the wide boulder-strewn river bank.

"This pool here is called Dreadnaught," said Hoka, pointing to a huge steep bluff strikingly like the shape of a dismantled man-of-war. It stood up all alone. The surrounding banks were low and green. After one glance, I gave my attention to picking my steps among the boulders, while Hoka kept on talking. "My people once fought battles here. They had a *pa* on top of this bluff. I'll show you graves that are wearing away. The skulls roll down into the river. Yes, my people, the Maoris, were great fighters. They stood up face to face, and gave blow for blow, like men."

At last I found a seat on a log, laid aside my rods, camera and coat, and looked up. I was interested in the Dreadnaught Pool, of course, but as I did not expect to catch a trout I did not feel my usual eagerness and thrills. The Captain probably would land one, but the few preceding days and the condition of the river had dashed my hopes. So I seemed a sort of contented idle comrade, agreeably aware of the music of the river, of the westering sun, of the sweet open space all about me, and the dark mountain range beyond.

I espied Captain Mitchell, pipe in mouth, rod in hand, tramping over the boulders to the head of the pool.

"Hey, Cap, what're you going to do?" I shouted.

"Fuinshh!" replied the Captain, whom you could never understand when he had that black pipe in his mouth.

Thus I was brought back to the motive of this climb, slide, and plow up to Dreadnaught Pool.

The Tongariro ran sweeping down in an S shape, between bright soft green banks; a white swift river, with ample green water showing, and rapids enough to thrill one at the idea of shooting them in a Rogue River boat. Not a canoe, thank you! The end of the last rapids piled against the hull of the Dreadnaugh bluff. A little rippling channel ran around to the right, out of sight, but it must soon have stopped, for the high embankment was certainly not an island.

I began to grow more than interested. The bluff had a bold bare face, composed of three strata; the lowest a dark lava studded thickly with boulders, the next and middle one a deep band of almost golden sand, and the topmost a gray layer of pumice in the top of which I saw the empty graves of the bygone Maoris.

The current deflected from the base of the bluff, sheered away and swept down through the pool, farther and farther out, until it divided into three currents running into three channels.

The lower and larger end of that pool grew fascinating to me. Under the opposite bank the water looked deep and dark. A few amber-colored rocks showed at the closer edge of the current. It shoaled toward the wide part, with here and there a golden boulder gleaming far under the water. What a wonderful pool! It dawned on me suddenly. The right channel, or one farthest over, ran glidingly under the curving bank, and disappeared. I could not see the level below. Points of rock and bars of boulders jutted out from a luxuriantly foliaged island. The middle channel was a slow wide shallow ripple, running far down. A low bare gravel bar rose to the left, and stretched to where the third channel roared and thundered in a deep curving rapid. Here most of the river rushed on, a deep narrow chute, dropping one foot in every three feet, for over a hundred yards.

I had to walk to the head of the rapid to see where the water ran, heaping up waves higher and higher, down the narrow channel that curved away under another high wooded bluff. This indeed was a green-white thundering Athabaska. Most of the water of the pool glided into the channel, growing swift as it entered. Green crystal water! I could see the bottom as plainly as if the depth had been ten inches instead of ten feet. How marvelously clear and beautiful! Round rocks of amber and gold and mossy green lay imbedded closely, like a color-ful tiling.

My gaze then wandered back over the head of the pool, where the Captain stood hip deep, casting far across into the current. And it wandered on down to the center, and then to the lower and wide part of the pool. What a magnificent place to fish! I made up swiftly for my lag-gard appreciation. I could see now how such a pool might reward a skillful far-casting angler, when the rain-bows were running. After a long climb up rapids, what a pool to rest in! There might even be a trout resting there then. So I picked up my rod and strode down to the river.

A clean sand bar ran out thirty yards or more, shelving into deep green water. Here a gliding swirling current moved off to the center of the pool, and turned toward the glancing incline at the head of the narrow rapid. The second and heavier current worked farther across. By wading to the limit I imagined I might cast to the edge of that bed water. I meant to go leisurely and try the closer current first. It was my kind of a place. It kept growing upon me. I waded in to my knees, and cast half across this nearer current. My big fly sank and glided on. I followed it with my eye, and then gave it a slight jerky movement. Darker it became, and passed on out of my sight, where the light on the water made it impossible for me to see. I had scarcely forty feet of line out. It straightened below me, and then I whipped it back and cast again, taking a step or two farther on the sand bar.

Then I had a look at Captain Mitchell. He was stand-ing with that pose of incomparable expectancy and patience. No use for me to try to imitate him! The tilt of his old black pipe demonstrated his utter contentment. Well, I thought, I did not have any pipe, because I never smoked; but I felt that I was just as contented as he.

Indeed I was not conscious of any other emotion. The fact that we were ahead of the running season for trout had operated to inhibit my usual thrill and excitement. It was the game to fish, to keep on trying, but I had not the slightest idea of raising a trout. If it had been otherwise I would have told Morton to be ready with a camera.

My line curved and straightened. Mechanically I pulled a yard or so off my reel, then drew perhaps twice as much back, holding it in loops in my left hand. Then I cast again, letting all the loose line go. It swept out, unrolled and alighted straight, with the fly striking gently. Was that not a fine cast? I felt gratified. "Pretty poor, I don't think," I soliloquized, and stole a glance upriver to see if the Captain had observed my beautiful cast. Apparently he did not know I was on the river. Then I looked quickly back at my fly.

It sank just at the edge of the light place on the water. I lost sight of it, but knew about where it floated. Suddenly right where I was looking on this glancing sunlit pool came a deep angry swirl. Simultaneously with this came a swift powerful pull, which ripped the line out of my left hand, and then jerked my rod down straight.

"Zee-eee!" shrieked my reel.

Then the water burst white, and a huge trout leaped in spasmodic action. He shot up, curved and black, his great jaws wide and sharp. I saw his spread tail quivering. Down he thumped, making splash and spray.

Then I seemed to do many things at once. I drew my rod up, despite the strain upon it; I backed toward the shore; I reeled frantically, for the trout ran upstream; I yelled for Morton and then for Captain Mitchell.

"Doc, he's a wolloper!" yelled the Captain.

"Oh, biggest trout I ever saw!" I returned wildly.

Once out of the water I ran up the beach toward Captain Mitchell, who was wading to meet me. I got even

with my fish, and regained all but part of the bag in my
line. What a weight! I could scarcely hold the six-
ounce rod erect. The tip bent far over, and wagged like
a buggy whip.

"Look out when he turns!" called Mitchell.

When the fish struck the swift current, he leaped right
before me. I saw him with vivid distinctness—the largest trout that I ever saw on line of mine—a dark bronze-
backed and rose-sided male, terribly instinct with the
ferocity and strength of self-preservation; black-spotted,
big-finned, hook-nosed. I heard the heavy shuffle as he
shook himself. Then he tumbled back.

"Now!" yelled Captain Mitchell, right behind me.

I knew. I was ready. The rainbow turned. Off like
an arrow!

"Zee! Zee! Zee!" he took a hundred yards of line.

"Oh Morton! Morton! . . . *Camera!*" I shouted
hoarsely, with every nerve in my body at supreme strain.
What would his next jump be? After that run! I was
all aquiver. He was as big as my big black Marlin. My
tight line swept up to the surface as I have seen it sweep
with so many fish. "He's coming out!" I yelled for Morton's benefit.

Then out he came magnificently. Straight up six feet,
eight feet and over, a regular salmon leap he made,
gleaming beautifully in the sun. What a picture! If
only Morton got him with the camera I would not mind
losing him, as surely I must lose him. Down he splashed.
"*Zee!*" whizzed my line.

I heard Morton running over the boulders, and turned
to see him making toward his camera. He had not been
ready. What an incomparable opportunity lost! I always missed the greatest pictures! My impatience and
disappointment vented themselves upon poor Morton,
who looked as if he felt as badly as I. Then a hard jerk

on my rod turned my gaze frantically back to the pool, just in time to see the great rainbow go down from another grand leap. With that he sheered round to the left, into the center of the wide swirl. I strode rapidly down the beach and into the water, winding my reel as fast as possible. How hard to hold that tip up and yet to recover line! My left arm ached, my right hand shook; for that matter, my legs shook also. I was hot and cold by turns. My throat seemed as tight as my line. Dry-mouthed, clogged in my lungs, with breast heaving, I strained every faculty to do what was right. Who ever said a trout could not stir an angler as greatly as a whale?

One sweep he made put my heart in my throat. It was toward the incline into the rapids. If he started down! But he ended with a leap, head upstream, and when he soused back he took another run, closer inshore toward me. Here I had to reel like a human windlass.

He was too fast; he got slack line, and to my dismay and panic he jumped on that slack line. My mind whirled, and the climax of my emotions hung upon that moment. Suddenly, tight jerked my line again. The hook had held. He was fairly close at hand, in good position, head upriver, and tiring. I waded out on the beach; and though he chugged and tugged and bored he never again got the line out over fifty feet. Sooner or later—it seemed both only a few moments and a long while—I worked him in over the sand bar, where in the crystal water I saw every move of his rose-red body. How I reveled in his beauty! Many times he stuck out his open jaws, cruel beaks, and gaped and snapped and gasped.

At length I slid him out upon the sand, and that moment my vaunted championship of the Oregon steelhead suffered an eclipse. The great Oregon rainbow, transplanted to the snow waters of the Tongariro, was superior in every way to his Oregon cousin, the silver-pink steelhead that had access to the sea. I never looked down upon such a magnificent game fish. No artist could have caught with his brush the shining flecked bronze, the deep red flush from jaw to tail, the amber and pearl. Perforce he would have been content to catch the grand graceful contour of body, the wolf-jawed head, the lines of fins and tail.

He weighed eleven and one-half pounds. I tied him on a string, as I was wont to do with little fish when a boy, and watched him recover and swim about in the clear water.

Meanwhile Morton stood there using language because he had failed to photograph those first leaps, and Captain Mitchell went back to his fishing. Presently a shout from him drew my attention. He had broken his rod on the cast.

"Well, what do you know about that?" I burst out. "If that isn't tough luck!"

The Captain waded out and approached us, holding two pieces of rod out for my inspection. The middle ferrule had broken squarely. While I tried to sympathize with Captain Mitchell, he anathematized the rod in several languages.

"But, Cap, you've had it for years. Even the best of rods can't last forever," I protested. "We'll take turn about using mine."

He would not hear of this, so I returned to fishing, with my three companions all on the *qui vive*. I thought to try the same water, and to save that wonderful space out there between the currents for the last.

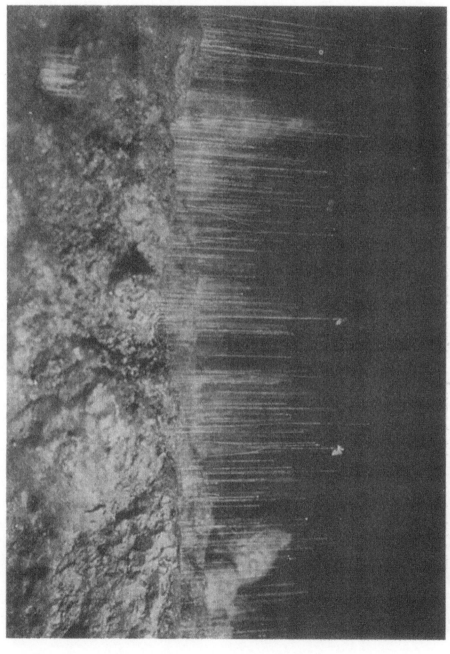

Some of the Beauties and Wonders of New Zealand (Plates xcviii to cxiii)

Plate xcviii

PLATE XCIX

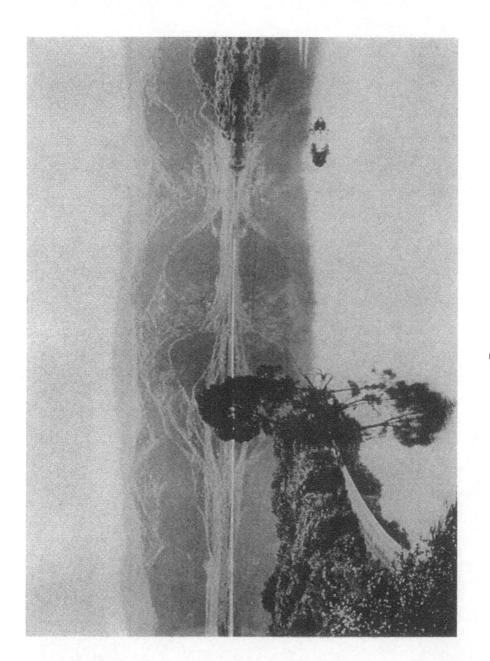

PLATE C

PLATE CI

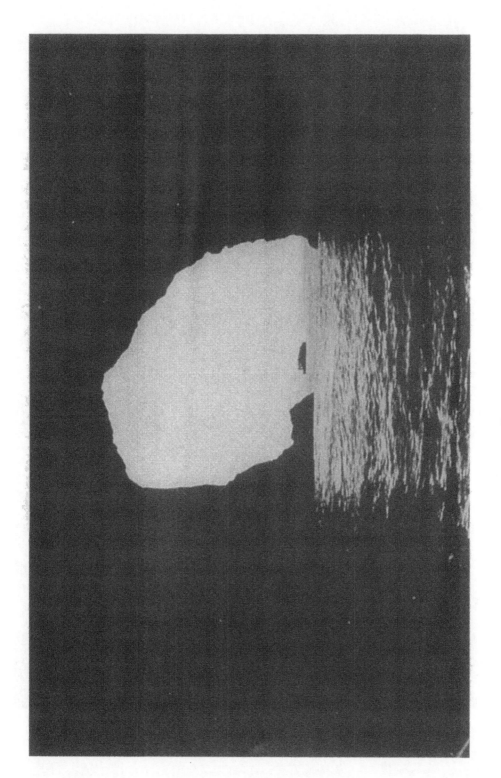

PLATE CII

PLATE CIII

PLATE CIV

PLATE CV

PLATE CVI

PLATE CVII

PLATE CVIII

PLATE CIX

PLATE CX

PLATE CXI

PLATE CXII

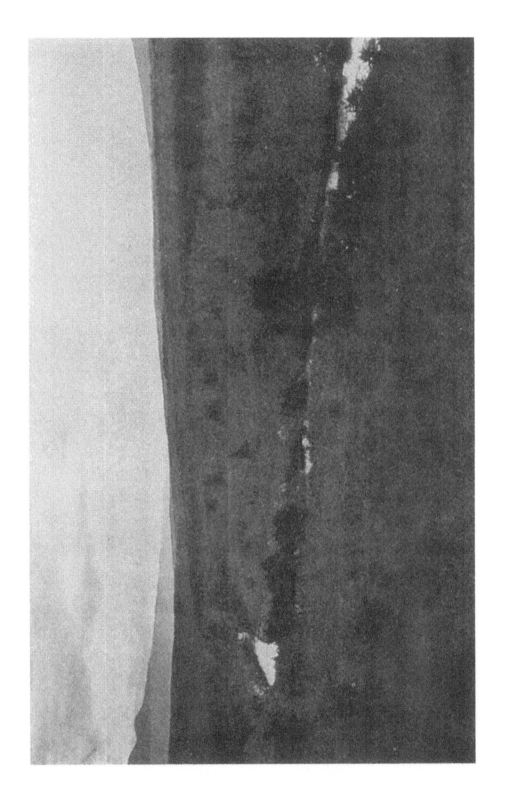

PLATE CXIII

CHAPTER XV

AS IF by magic of nature the Dreadnaught Pool had been transformed. The something that was ever-more about to happen to me in my fishing had happened there. There! The beautiful pool glimmered, shone, ran swiftly on, magnified in my sight. The sun was westering. It had lost its heat and glare. A shadow lay under the bluff. Only at the lower end did the sunlight make a light on the water, and it had changed. No longer hard to look upon!

I waded in up to my knees and began to cast with short line, gradually lengthening it, but now not leisurely, contentedly, dreamingly! My nerves were as keen as the edge of a blade. Alert, quick, restrained, with all latent powers ready for instant demand, I watched my line sweep out and unroll, my leader straighten, and the big dark fly alight. What singularly pleasant sensations attended the whole procedure!

I knew I would raise another rainbow trout. That was the urge, wherefore the pool held more thrill and delight and stir for me. On the fifth cast, when the line in its sweep downstream had reached its limit, I had a strong vibrating strike. Like the first trout, this one hooked himself; and on his run he showed in a fine jump—a fish scarcely half as large as my first one. He ran out of the best fishing water, and eventually came over the sand bar, where I soon landed him, a white-and-rose fish, plump and solid, in the very best condition.

"Fresh-run trout," said Hoka. "They've just come up from the lake."

"By gad! then the run is on," returned Captain Mitchell with satisfaction.

This second fish weighed five and three-quarter pounds. He surely had all the strength of an eight-pound steelhead in his compact colorful body. I was beginning to understand what the ice water of the Tongariro meant to the health and spirit of a rainbow.

"Cap, make a few casts with my rod while I rest and hug the fire," I said. "That water has ice beaten a mile."

"Not on your life," replied the Captain warmly. "I've a hunch it's your day. Wade in; every moment now is precious."

So I found myself out again on the sand bar, casting and recasting, gradually wading out until I was over my hips and could go no farther. At that I drew my breath sharply when I looked down. How deceiving that water! Another step would have carried me over my head. If the bottom had not been sandy I would not have dared trust myself there, for the edge of the current just caught me and tried to move me off my balance; but I was not to be caught unawares.

Sunlight still lay on the pool, yet cool and dark now, and waning. I fished the part of the pool where I had raised the two trout. It brought no rise. Then I essayed to reach across the gentler current, across the narrow dark still aisle beyond, to the edge of the strong current, sweeping out from the bluff. It was a long cast for me, with a heavy fly, eighty feet or more. How the amber water, the pale-green shadowy depths, the changing lights under the surface seemed to call to me, to assure me, to haunt with magical portent!

Apparently without effort, I cast my fly exactly where I wanted to. The current hungrily seized it, and as it floated out of my sight I gave my rod a gentle motion. Halfway between the cast and where the line would have straightened out below me, a rainbow gave a heavy and irresistible lunge. It was a strike that outdid my first. It almost unbalanced me. It dragged hard on the line I clutched in my left hand. I was as quick as the fish and let go just as he hooked himself. Then followed a run the like of which I did not deem possible for any fish short of a salmon or a Marlin. He took all my line except a quarter of an inch left on the spool. That brought him to the shallow water way across where the right-hand channel went down. He did not want that. Luckily for me, he turned to the left and rounded the lower edge of the pool. Here I got line back. Next he rushed across toward the head of the rapid. I could do nothing but hold on and pray.

Twenty yards above the smooth glancing incline he sprang aloft in so prodigious a leap that my usual ready shout of delight froze in my throat. Like a deer, in long bounds he covered the water, how far I dared not believe. The last rays of the setting sun flashed on this fish, showing it to be heavy and round and deep, of a wonderful pearly white tinted with pink. It had a small head which resembled that of a salmon. I had hooked a big female rainbow, fresh run from old Taupo, and if I had not known before that I had a battle on my hands I knew it on sight of the fish. Singularly indeed the females of these great rainbow trout are the hardest and fiercest fighters.

Fearing the swift water at the head of the rapid, I turned and plunged pellmell out to the beach and along it, holding my rod up as high as I could. I did not save any line, but I did not lose any, either. I ran clear to the end of the sandy beach where it verged on the boulders. A few paces farther on roared the river.

Then with a throbbing heart and indescribable feelings I faced the pool. There were one hundred and twenty-five yards of line out. The trout hung just above the rapid and there bored deep, to come up and thump on the surface. Inch by inch I lost line. She had her head upstream, but the current was drawing her toward the incline. I became desperate. Once over that fall she would escape. The old situation presented itself—break the fish off or hold it. Inch by inch she tugged the line off my reel. With all that line off and most of it out of the water in plain sight, tight as a banjo string, I appeared to be at an overwhelming disadvantage. So I grasped the line in my left hand and held it. My six-ounce rod bowed and bent, then straightened and pointed. I felt its quivering vibration and I heard the slight singing of the tight line.

So there I held this stubborn female rainbow. Any part of my tackle or all of it might break, but not my spirit. How terribly hard it was not to weaken! Not to trust to luck! Not to release that tremendous strain!

The first few seconds were almost unendurable. They seemed an age. When would line or leader give way or the hook tear out? But nothing broke. I could hold the wonderful trout. Then as the moments passed I lost that tense agony of apprehension. I gained confidence. Unless the fish wheeled to race for the fall I would win. The chances were against such a move. Her head was

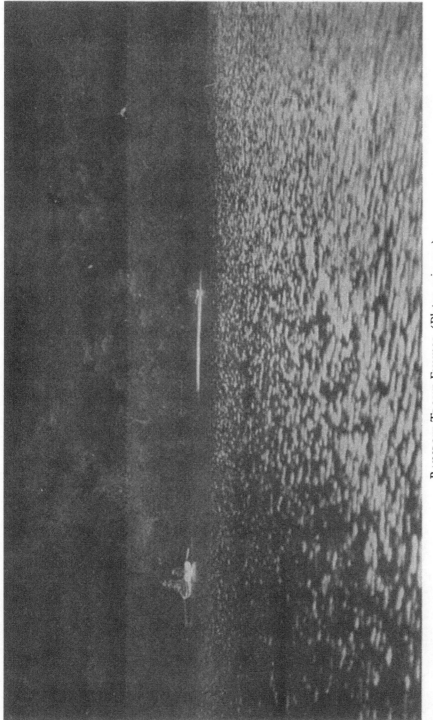

RAINBOW TROUT FISHING (Plates cxiv-cxx)
(*Mouth of the Waihoro River, Lake Taupo.*)

PLATE CXIV

PLATE CXVI

PLATE CXV

PLATE CXVII

PLATE CXVIII

PLATE CXIX

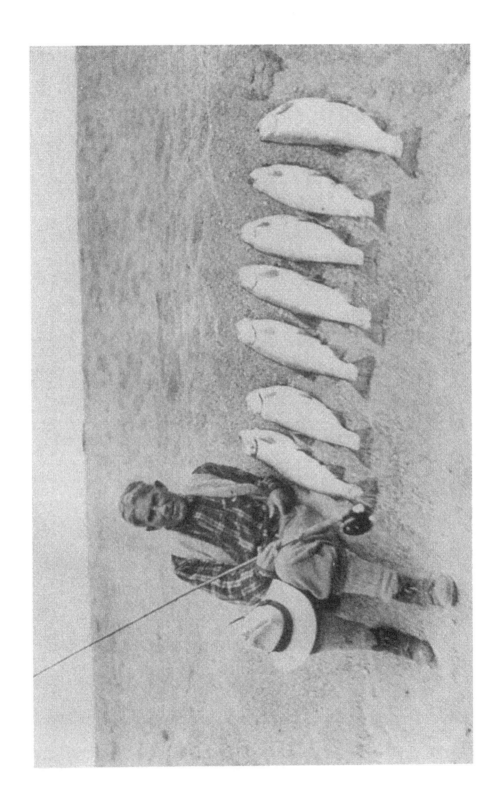

PLATE CXX

up current, held by that rigid line. Soon the tremendous strain told. The rainbow came up, swirled and pounded and threshed on the surface. There was a time then when all old fears returned and augmented; but just as I was about to despair, the tension on rod and line relaxed. The trout swirled under and made upstream. This move I signaled with a shout, which was certainly echoed by my comrades, all lined up behind me, excited and gay and admonishing.

I walked down the beach, winding my reel fast, yet keeping the line taut. Thus I advanced fully a hundred yards. When I felt the enameled silk come to my fingers, to slip on the reel, I gave another shout. Then again I backed up the beach, pulling the trout, though not too hard. At last she got into the slack shallow water over the wide sand bar.

Here began another phase of the fight, surely an anxious and grim one for me, with every move of that gorgeous fish as plain as if she had been in the air. What a dogged stubborn almost unbeatable fish on such tackle! Yet that light tackle was just the splendid thing for such a fight. Fair to the fish and calling to all I possessed of skill and judgment! It required endurance, too, for I had begun to tire. My left arm had a cramp and my winding hand was numb.

The fish made short hard runs out into the deeper water, yet each run I stopped eventually. Then they gave place to the thumping on the surface, the swirling breaks, the churning rolls, and the bulldog tug, tug, tug. The fight had long surpassed any I had ever had with a small fish. Even that of the ten-pound steelhead I hooked once in wild Deer Creek, Washington! So strong and unconquerable was this rainbow that I was fully a quarter of an hour working her into the shallower part of the bar. Every time the deep silvery side flashed, I almost had heart-failure. This fish would go heavier than the eleven-and-a-half-pound male. I had long felt that in the line, in the rod; and now I saw it. There was a remarkable zest in this part of the contest.

"Work that plugger in close where the water is shallower," advised Captain Mitchell.

Indeed, I had wanted and tried to do that, for the twisting rolling fish might any instant tear out the hook. I held harder now, pulled harder. Many times I led or drew or dragged the trout close to shore, and each time saw the gleaming silver-and-pink shape plunge back into deeper water.

The little rod wore tenaciously on the rainbow, growing stronger, bending less, drawing easier.

After what seemed an interminable period there in this foot-deep water the battle ended abruptly with the bend of the rod drawing the fish head on to the wet sand. Captain Mitchell had waded in back of my quarry, suddenly to lean down and slide her far up on the beach.

"What a bally fine trout!" burst out Morton. "Look at it! Deep, fat, thick. It'll weigh fourteen."

"Oh no," I gasped, working over my numb and aching arms and hands.

"By gad! that's a wonderful trout!" added the Captain, most enthusiastically. "Why, it's like a salmon!"

Certainly I had never seen anything so beautiful in color, so magnificent in contour. It was mother-of-pearl tinged with exquisite pink. The dots were scarcely discernible, and the fullness of swelling graceful curve seemed to outdo nature itself. How the small thoroughbred salmon-like head contrasted with the huge iron-jawed fierce-eyed head of the male I had caught first! It was strange to see the broader tail of the female, the thicker mass of muscled body, the larger fins. Nature had endowed this progenitor of the species, at least for the spawning season, with greater strength, speed, endurance, spirit and life.

"Eleven pounds, three quarters!" presently sang out the Captain. "I missed it a couple of pounds. . . . Some rainbow, old man. Get in there and grab another."

"Won't you have a try with my rod?" I replied. "I'm darn near froze to death. Besides I want to put this one on the string with the others and watch them."

He was obdurate, so I went back into the water; and before I knew what was happening, almost, I had fastened to another trout. It did not have the great dragging weight of the other two, but it gave me a deep boring fight and deceived me utterly as to size. When landed, this, my fourth trout, weighed six and three-quarters, another female, fresh run from the lake, and a fine rainbow in hue.

"Make it five, Doc. This is your day. Anything can happen now. Get out your line," declared Mitchell, glowing of face.

The sun had set as I waded in again. A shimmering ethereal light moved over the pool. The reflection of the huge bluff resembled a battleship more than the bluff itself. Clear and black-purple rose the mountain range, and golden clouds grew more deeply gold. The river roared above and below, deep-toned and full of melody. A cool breeze drifted down from upstream.

I cast over all the water I had previously covered without raising a fish. Farther out and down I saw trout rising, curling dark tails out of the gold gleam on the water. I waded a foot farther than ever and made a cast, another, recovered line, and then spent all the strength I had left in a cast that covered the current leading to the rising trout. I achieved it. The fly disappeared, my line glided on and on, suddenly to stretch like a whipcord and go zipping out of my left hand. Fast and hard!

What a wonderful thrill ran up and down my back, all over me!

"Ho! Ho! . . . Boys, I've hung another!" I bawled out, in stentorian voice. "Say, but he's taking line! . . . Oh, look at him jump! . . . Oh, two! . . . Oh, three! . . . Four, by gosh! . . . Oh, Morton, if we only had some sunlight! What a flying leapfrog this trout is! . . . *Five!*"

The last jump was splendid, with a high parabolic curve, and a slick cutting back into the water. This rainbow, too, was big, fast, strong and fierce. But the fish did everything that should not have been done and I did everything right. Fisherman's luck! Beached and weighed before my cheering companions; nine and one-half pounds; another silvery rosy female rainbow, thick and deep and wide!

Then I forced Captain Mitchell to take my rod, which he would not do until I pleaded I was frozen. But what did I care for cold? I made the day a perfect one by relinquishing my rod when I ached to wade in and try again.

The day, however, had begun badly for Captain Mitchell and so it ended. He could not raise a trout. Then we left the rousing fire and strode off over the boulders into the cool gathering twilight. Hoka carried two of my trout, Captain two, and Morton one. We threaded the *ti*-tree thicket and the jungle of ferns, and crossed the perilous panel in the dark, as if it had been a broad and safe bridge.

My comrades talked volubly on the way back to camp, but I was silent. I did not feel my heavy wet waders or my leaden boots. The afterglow of sunset lingered in the west, faint gold and red over the bold black range. I heard a late bird sing. The roar of the river floated up at intervals. Tongariro! What a strange beautiful high-

THE FALLS OF THE WAIHAHA (Plates cxxi to cxxiv)

PLATE CXXI

PLATE CXXIII

PLATE CXXII

Plate CXXIV

sounding name! It suited the noble river and the mountain from which it sprang. Tongariro! It was calling me. It would call to me across the vast lanes and leagues of the Pacific. It would draw me back again. Beautiful green-white thundering Tongariro!

I had three more memorable afternoons and sunsets at the Dreadnaught Pool. I saw Captain Mitchell raise and hook a big rainbow that leaped like a giant steelhead for the rapids, gain the fall and go over. I saw my comrade run plunging over the boulders, through the brush, down that steep bank, with a nodding rod extended far ahead of him. I did not follow, because I knew what must happen. Soon the Captain returned, to exhibit a broken leader. Also he exhibited a coolness and ease that I could never have maintained over such loss.

"By gad! wasn't that trout a buster?" was all the comment he made.

"Shades of the Rogue, Cap," I replied. "That bird was one of our old steelhead pards from Winkle Bar or Solitude."

Next day towards evening I had four fine strikes, standing in my favorite place on that pool, but I never hooked a fish. Then I gave way to the Captain, and while I hugged the warm fire he cast with his usual persistence. Reward came to him at length in the shape of a beautiful rise, a wonderfully striking fish, and then a spectacular fight with one of my big rainbows. The pool seemed now to be mine and all the trout; and I was as rich as if the sands were pearls, the water nectar and the rocks pure gold. I made Dreadnaught Pool mine through love, and I would possess it always through memory.

Captain's trout was one of the red-sided gaping-jawed males, nine and one-half pounds weight.

The following afternoon was one of singular charm along the river; golden, mellow, hazy, like Indian summer, with the fragrance of autumn and burning leaves in the air. It was to be my last try at the Tongariro for this trip—perhaps forever. *Quien sabe?* Seventy-five hundred miles was a long way to journey to fish, and life was uncertain. Here seemed the beauty and joy, the sting of adventure, the same as in boyhood. Ah! keener by far; and yet only a step away was the unknown future.

The goddess of fortune lingered kindly, however, on my trail. I had an hour of unalloyed angling joy, raising and fighting and landing three rainbows on the same big fly I had made myself. Six and one-half pounds, nine and one-quarter, and nine and three-quarter pounds all the pearly-white-and-rose females, game to the last!

Pride and vainglory were due for a jolt. I hooked the biggest rainbow of all, a heavy submarine fellow that would not leap, but plugged deep and hard. I never knew his size until I had him in the shallow water. Over twelve pounds, possibly fourteen! How he fought! What deep rose-red his long wide sides! The little six-ounce rod was quite equal to beating him, and so was the line; but I was not quite up to them. I foozled it, as the golfers say. I did something wrong, I knew not what, unless it was play him too long; and he wore out my leader. Free, away he swam, slow and weary, to vanish in the darkening purple of the pool.

Only a moment did I stand chagrined and dismayed; then I recovered. The loss of that most splendid of all the Tongariro rainbows I had hooked only heightened the glory of the whole adventure. Maybe I would raise him next year!

We trudged campward in the gloaming, under the

brightening stars. Wiffin and Morton and Captain and
Hoka were all happy over my good luck, and they were
gay. Something within me responded, though I needed
the silence and loneliness, to feel and ponder over this
last night on the Tongariro. We reached Hoka's land,
and as I tramped along with tackle and camera and my
biggest fish, I hit my heavy boot on a wire and fell head-
long over and over. My comrades haw-hawed their glee.
Then before I could rise, the Captain tripped as had I,
and what a fall he had! He hit on his back; and one of
my big trout, which he was carrying, flapped him squarely
in the face. So I had my laugh.

Through the trees shone the camp fires, and soon I
smelled the pungent wood smoke. How good the bright
blaze, the red embers, the pleasant heat! I changed into
warm dry clothes and was the first to squat Indian fashion
before the supper spread on a tarpaulin.

Soon I stole back to the quiet of the fire Hoka had
kindled before my tent. I sat there toasting my shins,
that the icy Tongariro had almost frozen. Then I walked
under the dark trees, and at last out to the high bank
above the river. What was this? Regret at the end of
a wonderful trip? I was a churl; but I hated to leave.
Soon the great rainbows would be running from the
depths of Lake Taupo up the swift river. How alluring
that thought!

"But I can come back!" I whispered to the river. "Tongariro, I will come back!" And it seemed the rushing
waters answered me. Thus I conquered longing and regret by sealing a compact with this Athabaska of the
Antipodes, by stealing happiness from the future, trans-
forming my whole mood. During the night I awoke
now and then, always to the dreamy roar of the river.
Once old Ngauruhoe let out a deep and moving rumble,

that rolled away under me, profound and tremendous, reminding me of the vain oblations of little man.

Bright and early next morning we broke camp, the Bakers to go one way and we the other. Fishermen must part. Baker's last words to the Captain and me were concerning the English tackle he would fetch us to Catalina in June. Forever anticipating—that is the true angler. I carried old Hoka's smile away with me. Bighearted, simple and sensitive, he sorrowed to see us leave, yet hid his grief under that smile. So might any man learn from the Maori! The last words he said were that his camp should henceforth be called Zane Grey Camp.

I did not look back. Only once more did my reluctant gaze catch sight of the Tongariro, green and swift under a wooded bend. The miles then brought me new evidence of the wonder of New Zealand. I rode under the shadow of Tongariro Mountain, green at the base with thick forest, belted above with the purple and bronze and yellow of denuded surfaces, and stark at the summit. Also I rode under the grand cone of Ngauruhoe, belching huge mushrooms of murky smoke high into the heavens. I saw the ragged open lips of the crater, and the zigzag bands of black lava running down the vast slopes. Ngauruhoe was active and too close for comfort. Yet how grand to gaze up at! Again rose that low strange rumble, almost roar, rolling up from the depths, terrific in its import.

Lastly we passed Ruapehu, the highest of the three great peaks. It was showing vast fields of snow that glistened in the sunlight. Those snowfields were the fountains from which sprang the cool pure Tongariro River. Somewhere on the other side of the splendid mountain the river had its source.

The whole scene was on a sublime scale. League on

league of rolling prairie-like land, almost gold in color, bare except for a green clump of forest here and there that accentuated the barrenness, swept up to the three noble peaks. All three were volcanoes. Tongariro smoked from several craters; Ngauruhoe sent aloft a grand column of steam and smoke; and Ruapehu lay asleep and cold, dead and extinct, or not yet responsive to the bursting fire and lava beneath.

This was the scene by which I chose to remember New Zealand. Land of mountains, ferns and crystal streams! Maori land, wild as any desert, verdant as any tropic jungle! Land of the Long Daylight!

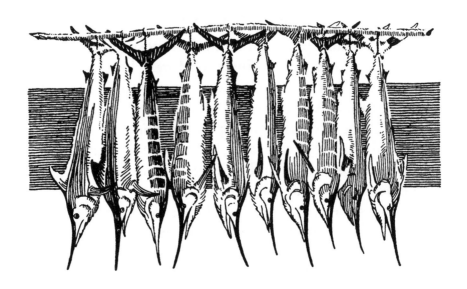

CHAPTER XVI

MY ENTHRALLMENT with Taupo and the Tongariro had put out of mind something disturbing, if not unfortunate, that had come to pass through my writing newspaper articles about the salt-water fishing at Cape Brett. The situation had developed into what newspapers and contributors called a controversy. Now I feel that I owe it to American anglers to explain the situation. So I shall begin by quoting, from my two articles in the *Auckland Herald*, the parts to which certain New Zealand fishermen took exception.

ORUPUKUPUKU ISLAND,
BAY OF ISLANDS,
February 10th.

. . . In my country salt-water fishing has been a development of fifty years. It has little to do with fresh-water fishing, absolutely nothing with what we call fly fishing. The tackle has been as much of a development as the method. Indeed the tackle is everything. An angler might be an expert at salt-water fishing, and the merest tyro at fresh-water angling, and *vice versa.*

It has been only of comparatively recent years that tackle suitable for the great tuna and swordfish has been manufactured, and in my case what I use is specially made for me.

Along with this development of tackle have mounted the ethics of the game. Certain weights of tackle were established for certain fish. Harpoons were prohibited. If one was found on an angler's boat his catches would be disqualified. The triple hook, or gang hook as we call it, was barred by all high-class angling clubs.

I want to say here that aside from the triple hook being un-sportsman-like, it is not in any way *so good* a hook as the single one. I have fished with live bait for many years, for bass, trout, perch, muskalonge, pike, catfish, and all the sea fishes, and always with a single hook, always hooked through the lips of the live bait. The reasons for this are too numerous to mention here. This is not merely my idea, but the practice of the best live-bait fishermen in the world. Perhaps I should add that the Japanese are the greatest of all fishermen. Well, they hook their live bait on a single hook, through the mouth.

Now as to the New Zealand tackle! In the pictures sent me I wondered how the anglers caught such big fish on long slim rods, with guides and reel underneath the rod. I could not understand it. I never understood it until I *saw* these rods used here at Cape Brett.

New Zealand anglers and Englishmen, in fact, all anglers who come here, have adopted the method that must have first developed. From a standpoint of American angling it is absolutely all wrong. I will try to explain, but that will be hard to do on paper.

At Russell, Mr. Caughey brought down his tackle for me to see. And I told him what I thought about it. But he did not agree with me until he got his hands on *my* tackle. Then he grasped the points hard to see.

It is impossible to fight a great game fish with reel and guides underneath the rod. I mean *stop* him and *fight* him. In order to do that an angler must have a short strong rod, one that will bend and spring back, a heavy reel with adequate drag, and powerful line. Reel and guides must be on top, because if they are not the angler cannot brace his feet on the boat and *pull* with all his might.

The New Zealand style of tackle is really an evolution from the English salmon tackle. English salmon and trout anglers and their tackle are the best in the world. But when it comes to salt-water tackle and methods, they have tried to develop along the same lines. The American tackle and method are so much the better that comparison is misleading.

Hardy Bros., of London, are now manufacturing rods modeled after the Tuna Club regulations; and also the "Alma" reel, which is a magnificent piece of work made under the supervision of Alma Baker, who is here fishing with me now. New Zealanders will eventually come to the use of this English made tackle, and have infinitely better sport and success.

At Cape Brett one day, I saw thirteen fish hooked, seven of which got away. I watched keenly with both naked eye and glass. The New Zealand angler, when he got a bite, merely held his rod up and let the boatman run the boat in the direction the fish wanted to go. He did not strike the fish hard, as we do. He did not bend the rod, or pump the fish, as we do. He followed the fish out to sea, and several hours later returned either with or without the fish, mostly without.

In connection with this, I want to make a point for the boatmen, who no doubt have not been valued fully for their work. In the method of following a fish until he is exhausted or dies of starvation, or comes up at last near the boat to be harpooned or gaffed, the credit always goes to the angler. But it is really the boatman who should have most of the credit.

In America, that method had its rise and fall. Many anglers hooked fish on tackle too light to stop them, but they followed them around for hours, eventually having the boatmen gaff them. Especially is this frowned upon in America in case of the broadbill swordfish, for he was sure to come to the surface sooner or later, to see what was dragging at him. Then he could be gaffed or harpooned long before the angler whipped him. In fact, many fish have been claimed by anglers who did not and could not whip them.

Of course, you can hook fish so big you *have* to follow them for a while. My seven-hundred-and-fifty-eight-pound record tuna made us follow him full speed for miles. But a fish should be stopped and fought.

One New Zealand boatman told me that out of twenty-four

FISHING THE QUIET WATERS (Plates cxxv to cxxx)

PLATE CXXV

PLATE CXXVI

PLATE CXXVII

Plate CXXVIII

PLATE CXXIX

PLATE CXXX

swordfish, three mako and one thresher, all caught by his boat, almost all of them were foul hooked. I also ascertained that missed strikes, broken lines and rods, hooks tearing out, etc. were regarded as incidentals of the day, and scarcely worthy of record. The triple or gang hook would account for the foul-hooking; and the indifference of anglers in the early stages of a new sport would account for the other.

Drifting for fish with live bait is as old as the hills. I learned that method as a boy. It is fishing, of course, and all fishing is wonderful, but it cannot be compared to trolling or casting. In trolling, you get the solid smash of the strike and see the fish; you hook him in the mouth, and that makes him jump. In reasonably smooth water, Marlin will rise. If the sea is calm I can raise Marlin here as well as elsewhere.

I have read, and heard, too, that this New Zealand swordfish does not jump, or breach, as the whalers call it. One of my Marlin leaped twenty-seven times, another twenty-six, another eighteen, another eleven. They were all hooked outside the mouth. The drifting method makes it almost impossible to hook a swordfish in the mouth.

ORUPUKUPUKU ISLAND,
March 14th.

After nearly two months fishing from Cape Brett to the Kara Kara Islands, Captain Mitchell and I have established a pretty accurate estimate of the extraordinary fighting qualities of the black Marlin swordfish and the mako.

I have caught ten mako to date, and the Captain about the same number. Up to four hundred pounds, this fish is immature, and often yielding. The large mako are torpedoes. Captain Mitchell hooked one yesterday we estimated to weigh twelve hundred pounds. It leaped prodigiously and made incredible runs, finally biting the leader through. This mako was truly terrific—the most wonderful fish either of us ever saw on a line.

As for the black Marlin swordfish, he is scarcely to be placed behind the mako. I hooked three large black Marlin that thoroughly outwitted me and escaped. Finally I had the luck to hold one, and after as hard a four-hour battle as I ever had with a fish, in which he punished me fearfully, I captured him. I killed him on the rod, but I am bound to confess he whipped me soundly. He leaped twelve times, a magnificent spectacle; and weighed seven hundred and four pounds.

A final word as to the tackle. I must add that in spite of the most expensive and powerful reels, lines and rods that have ever been built, I find we are not perfectly equipped to fight these great fish squarely and fairly. As for the tackle used here by New Zealand and English anglers, it is hopelessly inadequate, and unsportsman-like in the extreme. The triple hook is an abomination. I have absolutely ascertained that many of these giant swordfish are hooked in the stomach or throat with these gang hooks, and move off slowly and deeply out to sea, break off or tear loose, and die without the angler ever knowing what a marvelous fish he had on. By using a single hook we got a leaping fight out of these black Marlin.

New Zealand waters are undoubtedly the most remarkable in the Seven Seas for magnificent game fish. They will attract anglers from all the world. It behooves the sportsmen here to adopt the finest and fairest methods of angling; and it behooves the government to prohibit the dynamiting of schooling fish. There is no doubt that preservation of the fish and proper publicity will add immeasurably to New Zealand prosperity.

In reply to this latter article, a Mr. G. Buddle, of Auckland, published in the *Herald* a scathing and insulting letter which came rather as a surprise and shock to me.

I canceled the other articles I had been asked to write for the papers, and had no more to say. Alma Baker and Captain Mitchell both wrote long and instructive articles in defense of our tackle and methods, the most significant points of which the newspapers failed to print. Every day or so, another article would be published about the so-called controversy. Mr. Buddle published another letter, misquoting me, and showing his lack of understanding of what we did mean; and he went so far as to state that he had tried both kinds of tackle and methods of fishing, and had found the New Zealand kind superior. This amazing statement inspired me to inquire further, and I ascertained what I had divined—that no American rod, reel, line, or leader, with the single hook, nor the American method, had ever been used in New Zealand.

I am explaining these facts so there will be a definite record of them. The New Zealand coast is destined to become the most famous of all fishing waters. It will bring the best of anglers from all over the world. *Then* the question of right tackle and right method will be solved.

My visit to New Zealand was prompted by Alma Baker and the New Zealand government, who wanted me to come and fish and write for the benefit of the sport —to make it known to anglers all over the world. The importance of this and the zest and thrill with which it inspired me quite blinded me to the possibility that there might be New Zealanders who would not want me to do anything of the kind.

Many of them, however, I am happy to state, visited Captain Mitchell and me at our Camp of the Larks on beautiful Orupukupuku Island, and had us show our tackle and demonstrate its use. Several of these were anglers of long experience at Cape Brett. Peter Gardiner, of Kamo, was one of these, as I have mentioned elsewhere in this book; and he was keen and quick to appreciate the great superiority and sportsmanship of our tackle and method.

We wished particularly to have Mr. Andreas, the Australian angler who was at Deep Water Cove, visit us and see our rods, reels, lines, etc., and let us show him, for the sake of the sport, just what we had and how we used it. According to repute, Mr. Andreas was the champion of the Cape Brett anglers; and we hoped to win him away from the clumsy unsportsman-like tackle in vogue there. Alma Baker sent his boat to Deep Water

Cove to fetch Mr. Andreas; but Mr. Andreas refused to honor our camp with his presence.

So far as I was concerned, there was not and could not be any controversy over the triple hook and the reel underneath the rod for salt-water fishing. A controversy is something in which people take sides and dispute over what is the better of two recognized things. There is no ground for favoring the triple hook and the reel under the rod. They are impossible for modern angling. The triple hook is obsolete; it has gone with the hand-line and the harpoon. Also, the reel and line guides underneath the rod are wrong, for reasons that are too obvious even for argument. They are used only by anglers who have never seen any other kind, who have no conception of the wonderful progress of salt-water angling.

The latest development of the so-called controversy, just before I sailed from New Zealand, manifested itself in the following circular which was sent out by the Bay of Islands Swordfish and Mako Club.

BAY OF ISLANDS

SWORDFISH AND MAKO SHARK CLUB

RUSSELL, N. Z.

It has been suggested by Mr. Zane Grey, Captain Mitchell, Mr. C. Alma Baker and others who have been fishing with great success in New Zealand waters, that the Bay of Islands Swordfish and Mako Shark Club adopt the Single Hook instead of the Treble or Gang Hook for catching the Big Game Fish.

We are told that the Single Hook is adopted by other Overseas Fishing Clubs throughout the world, of which they say it is more sportsman-like; therefore

ARE YOU IN FAVOUR OF THE SINGLE HOOK?

OR

ARE YOU IN FAVOUR OF THE TREBLE OR GANG HOOK?

Your kind reply would be very much appreciated by our Club.

Yours faithfully,

E. C. ARLIDGE,

Hon. Secretary.

It would appear from the foregoing that the other important feature of our contention—the absolute necessity for the reel to be used on top of the rod so that a big fish could be fought fairly, had been disregarded wholly.

This circular was addressed only to members of the club, all of whom were advocates of the triple gang hook. It is my conviction that the single hook has but a slim chance of being chosen; but that will not keep these gentlemen from seeing some day what a remarkable difference there is between the sporting way and the other. They will not fail to observe how the swordfish hooked in the mouth with a single hook puts up a magnificent leaping fight, while the swordfish with the triple gang hook in his gullet does not leap or fight at all. He swims off slowly, deep down, and at length comes up himself or is drawn up choking and bloody, with his stomach hanging out, dead or almost dead.

It is no trick, and no sport, to catch a swordfish on a great big murderous triple hook. The merest novice can do it. A ten-year-old child can do it.

On our homeward trip Captain Mitchell and I had the

good fortune to meet a Mrs. Ellis, also a passenger on the *Tahiti*. She had been fishing at the Bay of Islands ten days after our departure. We had read in the newspapers about her remarkable catch of three swordfish in ne day, and we had heard otherwise about this much-heralded sporting achievement. Naturally both Captain Mitchell and I were keen to get her point of view. We were curious to learn *how* she had really caught these Marlin. She was a thoroughbred outdoor American woman, and though not robust she had caught tarpon and sailfish in Florida. She frankly told us about her fishing at Russell and gave me leave to quote her.

"I was terribly disappointed," she said. "I didn't see any sport in it at all. I had to use those miserable triple hooks and fish their drifting way. Of course I wanted to troll. But the captain of the *Marlin* said we could not have any luck trolling, that Mr. Zane Grey and Captain Mitchell had caught only very few swordfish trolling, which I learned later was not the truth, but a defense lie to save the high-priced gasoline. We had lots of bites from snappers, and in fact I couldn't tell the difference between a snapper bite and a swordfish bite; neither could Captain Warne. I caught three swordfish, and I must confess I don't see where any credit or record is due me. My swordfish did not jump or fight hard. Captain Warne took the rod from me at times and worked on the fish. The big swordfish—three hundred and forty pounds—came up very soon, with his stomach hanging out, a horrible sight. In fact my swordfish swallowed that brutal triple hook.

"It certainly was no fun or sport to catch those fish," she concluded, "and I can't understand why so much was made of it by Russellites and the newspapers. I did understand that the thing which counts with the boat-

men was to *get* the fish, great competition existing between the boatmen on number of fish 'caught by the boat,'
as they expressed it."

I was annoyed that Warne would misrepresent my
achievement in my own way of fishing—trolling—rather
than come out frankly and tell Mrs. Ellis that he did not
want to troll because trolling used up too much gasoline;
that Mr. Grey, besides paying the usual price per day for
his boats, paid extra for all the gasoline used during his
months of fishing; by which, incidentally, the boatmen
profited.

This accumulation of disturbing incidents should have
been anticipated. I realized that some one must be the
pioneer of modern tackle and fishing in New Zealand's
coastal waters; some one must upset the conservative
provincialism of the fishermen; some one had to make
himself disliked for criticizing their peculiar ways of
being happy; some one must be made the goat; and it
might just as well be I as anyone. I wanted only to serve
the turn of instruction and improvement. I wanted only
to help these anglers to enjoy vastly finer and more
thrilling and fairer sport.

At any rate, with Captain Mitchell's help I accom-
plished what the government wanted me to do, and what
my friends expected. We demonstrated what New Zealand waters can yield in the way of magnificent leaping
fish through many marvelous fights which are recorded
in wonderful still pictures and by a moving picture which
I guarantee will thrill even the layman.

In this connection, I want to give due credit to the
great Coxe reels, the Murphy hickory rods, the Swastika
lines and the Pflueger swordfish hooks, without which we
could never have had such an extraordinary fishing experience. Here follows a record of our catch:

PERSONAL RECORD, SEA ANGLING, NEW ZEALAND, 1926

Broadbill Swordfish	400 pounds	39–thread line
		First *Xiphias gladius* ever caught on rod in New Zealand.
Black Marlin	704 pounds	39–thread line
Yellowtail (or Kingfish)	111 pounds	36–thread line
		World Record
Striped Marlin Swordfish	450 pounds	36–thread line
		World Record

Mako		*Striped Marlin Swordfish*	
Pounds	Thread Line	Pounds	Thread Line
258	36	226	36
115	"	286	
200	"	250	"
300	39	284	39
56	36	275	36
160	"	268	39
220	"	230	36
160	"	300	39
260	39	208	36
250	36	224	"
298	39	234	"
199	36	240	"
120	"	258	"
160	"	278	39
175	"	250	36
150	"	292	39
180	"	280	36
		270	39
		230	36
		276	"

Reremai (or Sand Shark)			
Pounds	Thread Line	168	"
702	36	266	"
510	39	334	39
380	36	246	36
282	"	206	"
		272	"
		244	"

Yellowtail (or Kingfish)			
Pounds	Thread Line	306	39
58	36	264	36
62	"	380	"
68	"	216	"
70	9	242	"
78	36	212	"

THE GREEN-WHITE, THUNDERING TONGARIRO (Plates cxxxi to cxxxviii)
(Most famous of New Zealand trout waters.)

PLATE CXXXI

PLATE CXXXII

Plate cxxxiii

Plate cxxxiv

PLATE CXXXV

PLATE CXXXVI

PLATE CXXXVIII

Striped Marlin Swordfish

Pounds	Thread Line
250	"
305	39
260	36
250	"
200	39
320	36
282	"

RECORD OF CAPTAIN MITCHELL, NEW ZEALAND, 1926

Black Marlin 685 pounds 36–thread line

Black Marlin 976 pounds 36–thread line
World Record

Mako		*Striped Marlin Swordfish*	
Pounds	Thread Line	Pounds	Thread Line
294	39	192	39
299	"	218	36
297	"	254	39
180	"	234	36
165	"	268	39
180	36	199	36
		302	39
		286	36
Hammer-head		278	39
Pounds	Thread Line	350	"
350	39	293	36
395	"	311	"
		202	"
Reremai (or Sand Shark)		264	39
Pounds	Thread Line	310	36
500	36	268	"
460	"	254	39
350	"	236	"
		226	"
Yellowtail (or Kingfish)		236	"
Pounds	Thread Line	258	"
75	36		
80	"		
70	"		

After all, this phase of my trip to New Zealand fades to insignificance in the light of so much that was so splendid for me to experience and learn. Alas that I cannot find space here for full recounting.

I received hundreds of letters from all over New Zealand, welcoming Captain Mitchell and me to that Land of the Long Bright Day; and on departure, others anticipating our return. Of all the many letters and messages I received from New Zealand schoolboys and schoolgirls, I am selecting the following for publication. It is singularly expressive of the friendliness of my youthful readers; and its presence here in some measure will show the gratitude and appreciation I feel for them all. The author of these verses is Constance Wheeler, of Block House Bay, Auckland.

MY FAVOURITE AUTHOR

Oh to him, my man of writers
Did I gladly cheer
As I saw his pictures printed
In our Heralds over here.

'Twas said he'd come to fish
In our New Zealand water
'Twas said he is a sportsman
And a famous Western Author.

When I've walked the crowded pavements
And have looked in bookshops gay
With books by many authors,
Still my favourite is—Zane Grey.

Why? He writes on all the things I love—
The horses, plains, and heavens above,
The "Wild West" country, and cowboys galore—
If I went to Texas I'd "shore" see a score.

"Now at Russell in full swing
Zane Grey's fishing," hear me sing.
"Catching fishes big and small,
Every day a splendid haul.

And I hope he pulls in whales,
Great big whoppers by the tails,
Leaving Russellites a-crying
Cause the fishes there are dying."

Au revoir to you, Zane Grey;
Luck be yours in every way.
As you sail away from here,
Guess you'll hear the fishes cheer,
Till you come again next year.
Then, by jove, they'll all feel queer.

I found my books, mostly the 3/6 English edition, everywhere that we went, even in the remote Maori homes, far out in the bush; and I found them read to tatters. This surely was the sweetest and most moving of all the experiences I had; and it faced me again with the appalling responsibility of a novelist who in these modern days of materialism dares to foster idealism and love of nature, chivalry in men and chastity in women. Yet how potent the knowledge for renewed hope and endurance!

I had the pleasure of learning that I had inspired substantial Wellington men to the organization of a sporting club which was to further the advancement of hunting and fishing in New Zealand. This club is to bear my name, and to have comfortable lodge and cabins on Orupukupuku Island, boats and tackle of the most improved type, to have in mind the comfort and good sport of anglers from across the seas, and to develop along the highest ideals of angling sportsmanship.

With Captain Mitchell, I had the great honor of dining with the Prime Minister, and of telling him and the members of his Cabinet some stories of our fishing experiences, notably that one where the Captain verified one of the names I had bestowed upon him—Tackle

Buster—by breaking two rods on the same fish. How they enjoyed that story; but no more than the Captain himself!

It was from the lips of Sir Maui Pomare, one of the Ministers of the government, that at last I heard the legend of Maui, the great Maori fisherman. Sir Maui bore that title himself, and in his blood ran the blood of those old Maori men of the sea.

Maui was the last born of five brothers. His mother, Taranga, displeased that Maui had been born prematurely, cut off the top of her hair and wrapping him in it she threw him into the sea.

The great god of the waters, seeing Maui consigned to the depths, took pity upon him and rescued and nourished him. Maui lived and grew in the abysmal caverns of the ocean, where all the finny tribes were known to him. It was here that Maui acquired his supernatural knowledge of the fishes of the Seven Seas.

When Maui arrived at man's estate, he longed to go back to the land to see his mother Taranga, and his brothers, and especially his sister whom he loved best of all. The great sea god cast him up from the waves to the golden sands. Whereupon Maui went to his old home and crawled in with his brothers.

When morning came, Taranga, as always, counted her sons: "Maui-taha, one. . . . Maui-roto, two. . . . Maui-pae, three. . . . Maui-waho, four."

Then espying her last born Maui, she cried out: "Hollo! where did this fifth man come from!"

"I'm your son, too," said Maui.

"Come, you be off now," she replied angrily. "You are no son of mine."

"Indeed, I was your child," said Maui. "Because I

know I was born by the side of the sea, and was thrown by you into the foam of the surf, after you had wrapped me in a tuft of your hair. The seaweed formed and fashioned me; the ever-heaving surges of the sea rolled me and folded me; the great sea god nurtured me and I became the playmate of fishes. I grew to be a man and longed for home. Here I stand before you, Taranga, my mother. You are my first-born brother, Maui-taha; and you are Maui-roto, and you are Maui-pae, and you are Maui-waho."

Then Taranga cried out: "You are indeed my last born, the son of my old age. You shall be Maui-tiki-tiki-a-Taranga, or Maui-formed-in-the-topknot-of-Taranga."

Maui was henceforth called by that name, and he became famous as a man of magic and enchantments. His brothers feared him, and were jealous, for Maui performed many wonderful feats.

Maui found that the daylight was too short for him to fish in, and the nights too short for sleep. No sooner did he awake than he had to go to bed again. So he took his brothers with him and traveled far to the east, to where the sun went to sleep at night; and in the morning when the sun awoke and began to stretch his arms, Maui and his brothers threw nooses around the sun and tangled him. Then Maui beat the sun so terribly that never again could he make the days and nights so short.

Best of all Maui loved to fish. All his brothers were good fishermen and his brother-in-law, the husband of his beloved sister, was the greatest of all fishermen. Despite the magic Maui exercised, he could not catch as many fish as his brother-in-law. Accosting his brother-in-law one day, he persuaded him to be allowed to accompany him.

They went out to sea, where Maui, fishing with all his magic, could not catch near so many fish as his brother-in-

law.   He contrived presently to tangle his line with the
other and draw it up at the same time his brother-in-law
drew his.

"The fish is on my line," said Maui.

"No.   It's on mine," replied his brother-in-law.

Maui, being the stronger, got the fish in first.   It was
indeed on his brother-in-law's hook, which had a barb of
human bone on it.   That barb was the secret of his
brother-in-law's wonderful fishing, and Maui felt that
he must have that hook.   So when they got ashore he said
to his brother-in-law:

"You get under that outrigger and help me lift the
canoe."

When his brother-in-law complied, Maui put his foot
on the outrigger and shoved him under the water.   Then
when his brother-in-law was helpless Maui with his
magic made him the ancestor of all the dogs in the world.

With the secret barb hook Maui next endeavored to
go out fishing with his four brothers.   This was a difficult
matter, for Maui's brothers did not want him.   They
feared his enchantments.   But one night Maui hid under
the deck of the great fishing canoe, and stayed there till
his brothers paddled off next morning.   When they were
out at sea, Maui slipped over the side and showed himself.   His brothers were much concerned and would not
anchor at their favorite fishing grounds.

"Let us go far out to sea," said Maui.

They paddled far out, and wished to drop anchor, but
Maui made them go still farther.   At last Maui was content to stop and fish, but he had no bait, and when he
asked his brothers for some, they said:

"No.   We will not give you any of our bait."

Whereupon Maui drew blood from his own nose, and
when it had congealed he put it on his secret barb hook.
Then he let it down into the sea.   His brothers could not

catch any fish. The waters were too deep. But Maui had a great strike, and by his secret hook and his magic and his strength of a giant he drew up the greatest fish ever caught by god or man—the North Island of New Zealand.

We sailed at four o'clock, April twenty-seventh, on the S.S. *Tahiti;* and when we steamed out of the bay the sun was setting over the dark mountain ranges. The sea was rough, white-crested, with spindrift flying like thistle down. A track of shimmering gold widened across the bright waters into the sunset. Beautiful New Zealand! Faraway Land! Fernland! Land of the Long Afternoons! How could I give it the most deserving name?

I gazed over those bold clear-cut ranges toward the north, where I had left the Kara Kara Islands and the Cavallis, and far to the interior, the green-white Tongariro River. How strange to love places so quickly! But love is not a matter of time. Again I wondered if I would ever come back. How many lovely places in the world to find and know! How many millions of lovely places one can never see! Albatross were following the steamer. With a quick break of emotion and a lively thrill I sighted the great sea birds, seven of them, some near and others far, sailing, floating, sweeping, soaring, swooping in the turbulent wake of the *Tahiti.*

I could not have asked more. The sun shone brighter as it tipped the range, and the albatross crossed that golden track of light over the sea. Shining black and white as they wheeled in their graceful gyrations. How wonderful indeed was that swoop when a great bird turned almost upside down, the tip of one vast wing skimming the waves and the tip of the other pointing to the sky!

They belonged to the far southern seas, to the Antarctic. Cold-miened, sleek-feathered, ponderous fowl of the Ancient Mariner! One of them, with a twelve-foot spread of wings, sailed toward and over me where I leaned on the stern rail. Like snow, his breast; and his long curved wings were the same, with an edging of black. I could see his yellow beak, his bleak uncanny eye. What power, what grace! He did not fly. He did not move his wings. He rested on the wind. Then he wheeled and like a thunderbolt swooped down, and away, over the billows on and on, and up again, grander than an eagle—the Wandering Albatross.

Through sunset and twilight and dark, while the steamer throbbed and water roared, I watched these sea birds until they and the dim receding land faded in the darkness of night.

THE END

Lightning Source UK Ltd.
Milton Keynes UK
UKHW031439060220
358278UK00007B/1195